Defining
Moments

Defining Moments

When Managers Must
Choose between
Right and Right

Joseph L. Badaracco, Jr.

HARVARD BUSINESS SCHOOL PRESS
BOSTON, MASSACHUSSETTS

Printed in the United States of America
04 03   12 11

Library of Congress Cataloging-in-Publication Data

Badaracco, Joseph.
    Defining moments : when managers must choose between right and
right / Joseph L. Badaracco, Jr.
        p.   cm.
    Includes bibliographical references and index.
    ISBN 0-87584-803-6
    1. Business ethics.   2. Executives—Professional ethics.
I. Title.
HF5387.B32   1997
174'.4—dc21   97-17613
                                                                    CIP

*The paper used in this publication meets the requirements of the American National
Standard for Permanence of Paper for Printed Library Materials Z39.49-1984.*

For Pat

Contents

Preface

Several years ago, I listened closely as a promising young manager at a well-known consumer products company described a difficult conflict between her responsibilities at work and her personal values. Later, after the issue was resolved, she drew several lessons from her experience, and one of them has stuck in my mind:

> *It was a wake-up call in a lot of ways—definitely on how organizations work. You can get stranded alone. I learned that you alone are responsible for yourself, for your personal and professional development.*

This statement is both realistic and distressing. Managers do get stranded. The experience can be painful and difficult. But when it happens, are they entirely alone? Where can they turn for guidance on the moral dilemmas of management?

For years, I found it difficult to answer these questions, even though I was teaching courses on leadership, management, and business ethics. Several standard answers were available—follow the law, serve the shareholders, consult the company credo, serve all the stakeholders, do the right thing—but these, I found, had limited practical value. Each of the standard answers contains an important element of truth, but all of them are abstract and very general. They float serenely above the messy, complicated, anxiety-laden, political dilemmas that managers must sometimes resolve, typically with too little time and information.

What managers value is guidance with traction, guidance that directly engages and illuminates their problems—*as they actually experience these problems*. I have now come to believe, after listening to hundreds of managers discuss difficult decisions of personal and professional responsibility, that the most useful guidance involves asking questions, not giving answers.

My search for the right questions led to writing this book, but by a peculiar path. I found that the most challenging, penetrating, and practical questions fused elements from an unusual range of sources. These included detailed case studies of business managers; enduring works of literature, like the classic portrayal of character and commitment in the Greek tragedy *Antigone*; contemporary fiction, like the story of the dutiful butler in the novel *The Remains of the Day*; the writings of tried-and-true philosophers, such as Aristotle; and the insights of supposed ethical renegades, particularly Machiavelli and Nietzsche.

At the heart of this book is a framework of questions drawn from these disparate sources. It is intended to provoke and to challenge: to elicit answers, not announce them. Above all, it is designed to help managers avoid the hazards of being "stranded alone"—by helping them frame thoughtful, practical, personally meaningful ways of resolving the inescapable dilemmas of life and work.

I am grateful to many friends and colleagues for their thoughtful contributions to the ideas presented in this book. I am particularly indebted to Ken Andrews, Colyer Crum, Bill Levin, George Lodge, Scotty McLennan, Tracy Mehan, Lynn Paine, Tom Piper, Amy Sandler, Howard Stevenson, Dennis Thompson, Tom Urban, Jerry Useem, and Abe Zaleznik. Nikki Sabin provided valuable guidance throughout the editorial process, as did Carol Franco and Rafe Sagalyn at its beginning. John Donovan provided a splendid opportunity to test and refine the ideas presented here.

I am particularly indebted to my friend Ken Winston for his many careful, judicious, and insightful suggestions. And, above all, I am deeply grateful to my wife, Pat O'Brien, whose perceptive, realistic, insightful ideas shaped every aspect of this book.

The Harvard Business School also deserves credit. The School's generous alumni, particularly the late John Shad, provided the resources that made the work possible. Over the years, MBA students and executives in my courses have taught me many important lessons about managers, their work, and their responsibilities. Deans John McArthur and Kim Clark, along with heads of the Division of Research, provided time for this endeavor, and my assistant, Bonnie Green, helped me protect this time and focus on the project.

I also owe a debt to several scholars, whose writings served as my guides to the moral philosophers discussed in this book. I relied on Stuart Hampshire, Alasdair MacIntyre, and Martha Nussbaum for Aristotle; Isaiah Berlin for Machiavelli; John Murphy and Richard Rorty for William James; Alexander Nehamas for Nietzsche; and Brand Blanshard for Marcus Aurelius. In the end, of course, the interpretations presented here are mine, as are any errors.

Brookline, Massachusetts
May 12, 1997

1

↔

Dirty Hands

*T*HOUGHTFUL MANAGERS sometimes face business problems that raise difficult, deeply personal questions. In these situations, managers find themselves wondering: Do I have to leave some of my values at home when I go to work? How much of myself—and of what I really care about—do I have to sacrifice to get ahead? When I get to the office, who am I?

Difficult questions like these are often matters of right versus right, not right versus wrong. Sometimes, a manager faces a difficult problem and must choose between two ways of resolving it. Each alternative is the right thing to do, but there is no way to do both.

Consider, for example, the problem faced by Rebecca Dennet, a branch manager for a major bank. Her boss, a senior executive, told her that her branch would be shut down in two months, shortly after the first of the year. The executive asked Dennet to keep the information confidential because important regulatory papers had yet to be filed, and she agreed to do so.

Two days later, a coworker asked Dennet if she knew anything about the rumor that the branch would soon be closed. When she hesitated, the coworker grew impatient and said, "Look, this is serious. There aren't a lot of jobs around here. Do I cut back on Christmas gifts? Do you know anything?"

What should Dennet have done? The right thing, of course, was to answer the question honestly—after all, she did know something. It is also right to be loyal to friends, and the woman asking for help and guidance was a good friend. But saying nothing was also right. As a corporate officer, Dennet's duty was to maintain confidentiality, and she had explicitly promised to do so. Clearly, her choice was not between right and wrong, but between right and right.

Rebecca Dennet's problem is hardly unique. Although the details differ, good managers often struggle with some version of this predicament. They want to live up to their personal standards and values, they have to meet the expectations of their customers and shareholders—often in the face of relentless profit pressures—and their own jobs are the foundation of their families' security. Most managers also want to be fair to the people who work for them, lend a hand to people in need, earn the respect of their families and friends, and maintain their personal integrity.

Most of the time, managers find ways to juggle all these responsibilities and aspirations. In some cases, however, they cannot. Then these responsible, successful, achievement-oriented people face the prospect of a serious kind of personal failure: the failure to live up to the commitments they have made and the standards by which they want to live. For managers who struggle with these kinds of situations, the stakes are very high. They go to the heart of what it means to be successful manager and a decent, responsible person.

CRUCIBLES OF CHARACTER

Situations like Rebecca Dennet's are sometimes called "dirty hands" problems. This peculiar name comes from the title of a play by the French philosopher Jean Paul Sartre. The story takes place in wartime. Its main characters include the veteran leader of an underground unit of the Communist party and a zealous young party member. At a crucial moment in the drama, the young man accuses his leader of betraying the party's ideals, through the compromises he has made with reactionary political forces.

The older man answers this harsh accusation in the following words:

> *How you cling to your purity, young man! How afraid you are to soil your hands! All right, stay pure! What good will it do? Why did you join us? Purity is an idea for a yogi or a monk. . . . To do nothing, to remain motionless, arms at your side, wearing kid gloves. Well, I have dirty hands. Right up to the elbows. I've plunged them in filth and blood. But what do you hope? Do you think you can govern innocently?*[1]

Do you think you can govern innocently? This is a powerful, haunting question, to which we will return at several points in this book. For now, however, the question has a single, clear, disturbing implication. The old Communist suggests that men and women who have power over the lives and livelihoods of others must almost inevitably get their hands dirty—not in the sense of rolling up their sleeves and working hard, but in the sense of losing their moral innocence.

For Rebecca Dennet and other managers, the question is: Do you think you can manage innocently? The veteran party leader poses the question in a way that reveals his answer. Only the naive, he believes, think that leaders can avoid dirty hands. But is this so? Are dirty hands really the inevitable lot of successful men and women with real power and responsibility in life? The Communist is a political leader in wartime. What does he have in common with a business manager?

Consider the reflections of Chester Barnard. Although few people know his name, Barnard was among this century's most insightful observers of business leaders. He combined an incisive mind with years of hands-on management experience to write *The Functions of the Executive*, a classic of management literature. First published in 1938, the book remains in print after more than 40 editions.

For many years, Barnard lived a remarkable double life. He spent his weekdays as the president of the Bell System in New Jersey, at a time when the phone company was a leading high-technology company. He spent evenings and weekends writing his masterwork on leadership and organization.

Barnard discusses managers' responsibilities at length. At one point, he makes an observation as remarkable and disturbing as the old Communist's. "It seems to me inevitable," Barnard warns, "that the struggle to maintain cooperation among men should as surely destroy some men morally as battle destroys them physically."[2]

This passage is remarkable as much for Barnard's realism as for the strength of his convictions. Management is not, for Barnard at least, the upbeat adventure described in many management books. It is the "struggle" to get people to work together. Moreover, he views his troubling conclusion as a dead certainty, calling it "inevitable."

Even more striking is the similarity between Barnard's conclusion and the view that Sartre expresses through the old Communist. Both men believed that positions of leadership impose difficult personal challenges that can destroy some men and women and strengthen others. For Barnard, leadership brings the risk of moral destruction. For Sartre, it raises the prospect of "dirty hands." Both men believed, in essence, that positions of leadership are crucibles of character.

How did two such different men—an American business executive and a French existentialist philosopher—come to share this conclusion? Part of the answer is that both were deeply engaged in the same quest: the effort to learn the bottom facts about the lives and decisions of individuals who have power over others and struggle at times with their responsibilities.

The other part of the answer is best understood by looking at the origins of dilemmas like Rebecca Dennet's. Positions of power carry complicated responsibilities. On some occasions, these responsibilities conflict with each other. At other times, they conflict with a manager's personal values. All of these responsibilities, personal and professional, have strong moral claims, but often there is no way for a manager to meet every claim. These are not the ethical issues of right and wrong that we learn about as children. They are conflicts of right versus right.

Neither Barnard nor Sartre believed that right-versus-right conflicts were purely intellectual issues. They knew that choices between right and right are fraught with personal risk. In these cases, when managers do one right thing, they leave other right things undone. They feel they are letting others down and failing to live up to their standards. The loss of innocence seems real, their hands feel dirty, and sometimes the moral calamity that Barnard warned of seems all too close.

Right-versus-right conflicts become questions about life and not just management for another reason: their finality. Once Rebecca Dennet makes a decision and implements it, there will be no turning back. She will have written a paragraph or a page of her personal and professional autobiography. Her choices will be recorded, not on a word processor that permits endless revisions, but in life's permanent record.

Right-versus-right issues are troubling, complicated, and serious. They are also too important to ignore. Good people in management jobs must sometimes make very hard choices. At issue is what it means to be a successful manager and a thoughtful, responsible human being. On this, Barnard and Sartre agree. So, too, would countless thoughtful managers, who struggle to balance their conflicting obligations in responsible, practical ways.

BEYOND INSPIRATIONAL ETHICS

This book examines the right-versus-right conflicts that every business manager faces. It presents an unorthodox and pragmatic way to think about these conflicts and resolve them. For managers, right-versus-right decisions are uniquely important choices. They can have powerful and often irrevocable consequences for the lives of the men and women who must make the decisions and for their organizations as well.

The approach presented here parts company with the standard inspirational answers to hard management problems. Most managers have heard the speeches in which executives champion a corporate credo or mission statement and exhort everyone to "Do the right thing." These speeches serve a useful purpose. They are usually sincere, some are genuinely inspiring, and they may even keep some employees on the straight and narrow.

But the inspirational approach offers little help with serious conflicts of responsibility. The truly difficult question is the one that Barnard and Sartre raise: What to do when one clear right thing must be left undone in order to do another or when doing the right thing requires doing something wrong? For managers, these problems are especially complex. Their right-versus-right problems typically involve choices between two or more courses of action, each of which is a complicated bundle of ethical responsibilities, personal commitments, moral hazards, and practical pressures and constraints.

Inspirational ethics usually avoids problems like these. It also ignores Barnard's warning and the problem of dirty hands. Uplifting platitudes ring hollow for these issues. They lead to deep and turbulent ethical waters. The question of right versus right sometimes reminds managers of difficult experiences of their own, which they would rather not recall because they involve feelings of failure, guilt, or loss. The question Do you think you can govern innocently? is unsettling, emotionally and intellectually. Our natural reaction is to respond yes, but this contradicts our experience.

Yet, to make progress on these issues, one must begin by looking them in the face. This is not a simple matter. The first step is to examine the basic kinds of right-versus-right problems that managers must solve. The next chapter does this through detailed accounts of problems facing three different managers.

The second step is to understand, in depth, why right-versus-right conflicts are so difficult. Much of the time, we think about problems in terms of unexamined categories, the familiar little boxes that we use to sort problems—as legal issues, business ethics issues, management issues, and so on. And, once we put a problem in the right box, we think we have the tools for solving it. But right-versus-right choices can't be forced into familiar categories, and they evade standard solutions. Neither Barnard nor Sartre would have dwelt on the problem of conflicting responsibilities if the answer were a simple matter of finding the right category and applying the right concepts.

This book argues that right-versus-right choices are best understood as *defining moments*. These are decisions with three basic characteristics: they reveal, they test, and they shape. In other words, a right-versus-right decision can reveal a manager's basic values and, in some cases, those of an organization. At the same time, the decision tests the strength of the commitments that a person or an organization has made. Finally, the decision casts a shadow forward. It shapes the character of the person and, in some cases, the organization.

THE URGENT QUESTIONS

For managers, the urgent questions are: How do I think about defining moments? How do I resolve them in ways I can live with? This book offers practical advice for reflecting on right-versus-right conflicts and finding ways to resolve them. In exploring three such conflicts in depth, it provides a framework for thinking through these difficult decisions.

The framework consists of a series of phrases and questions, each with deep roots in classic and contemporary moral philosophy. The questions encourage reflection, evoke personal perspectives and experiences, and invite self-assessment. They challenge managers to reflect on their relationships with people at work, at home, and in their communities. Each of these phrases and questions is based on a powerful idea about life and work, but readers must meet them halfway in order to understand and apply them. In other words, this approach to difficult choices does not stand at a lectern and tell people what to do. Instead, each question or phrase taps people on the shoulder, surprises them a bit, and then suggests a way of reflecting on some important aspect of their lives and their work.

The "dirty hands" passage offers a glimpse of this approach to ethical problems. "Dirty hands" is not simply a colorful phrase. Nor is it intended as a snapshot summary of Sartre's philosophy. And, although it can be the focus of rigorous philosophical analysis, that is not its role here.[3]

"Dirty hands" often reminds people of difficult episodes in their lives. So, too, does the question Do you think you can govern innocently? The phrase and the question can evoke memories, images, experiences, and feelings. They may also awaken abiding feelings of remorse about ethical failures or give people a sense of hard-won pride as they recall moral struggles they have handled well. This personal perspective is doubly valuable. It encourages people—whether managers or not—to reflect on their own lives and experiences. At the same time, it gives them an empathic view, a view from the inside, of what is at stake when managers and others must resolve serious conflicts among their responsibilities.

2

↔

Right versus Right

THIS CHAPTER INTRODUCES THREE MANAGERS and the right-versus-right conflicts they faced. Each is drawn from actual experience. Taken together, they illustrate the basic types of right-versus-right dilemma. The three cases also reveal the basic elements of the problem Rebecca Dennet confronted, and which other managers often must resolve.

Although the three cases differ in important ways, they all illustrate a dramatic statement made by Oliver Wendell Holmes, one of the most distinguished American Supreme Court justices. Holmes wrote, "I do not give a fig for the simplicity on this side of complexity, but I would give my life for the simplicity on the other side of complexity."

All three of the managers described here would have understood what Holmes was saying. All urgently needed practical answers to difficult problems. All would have preferred simple answers, such as "Do the right thing." But Barnard's warning about the moral hazards of management life applied in all three cases, and each manager faced the prospect of dirty hands.

CRISES OF MORAL IDENTITY

The first case involves a young man, Steve Lewis, who had just completed his first year of work at a prestigious New York investment bank. Lewis was an analyst, which meant that he spent his days and many of his nights dissecting detailed financial data. The rest of his life he described as "indoor camping." The refrigerator in his apartment was usually empty, he had hung nothing on the walls, and his living room furnishings consisted mainly of unpacked boxes. Nevertheless, Lewis told his friends, with whom he stayed in touch via email messages sent from the office, that he had the best job in the world.

Early one Tuesday morning, Lewis found a message on his desk asking whether he could fly to St. Louis in two days to help with a presentation to an important prospective client. The message came as a surprise to him. Lewis's firm had a clear policy against including analysts in presentations or client meetings, because they lack both experience and expertise. Lewis, in fact, knew little about the subject of the St. Louis meeting, a specialized area of municipal finance. He was especially surprised that he had been selected over several more senior people in the public finance group.

Lewis immediately walked down the hall and into the office of Andrew Webster, a friend and partner at the firm. He showed Webster the note and asked, "Andy, what's the deal here? Did you know I've been asked to go to the orals? Are you behind this?"

Webster interrupted him. "Let me tell you what's happening, my friend. Look at you and me. What similarities are there? Let me tell you that the new state treasurer of Missouri is also black." Webster continued, "Listen, Steve, I hate for you to be introduced to this side of the business so soon. The state treasurer wants to see at least one black professional, or the firm has no chance of being named a manager for this deal. I'm used to these situations, but if you feel uncomfortable with it, maybe you don't have to go. I could try to change my schedule and go instead of you."

Lewis quickly replied, "No, no. Don't do that. Let me just think it over. I'll get back to you." When Webster asked what the issue was, Lewis said he wasn't sure there was one. He thanked Webster and headed back to his desk.

Lewis spent several minutes answering his email, got a cup of coffee, made a list of things to do during the day, and finally realized that he was avoiding a decision on the St. Louis trip. He understood the issue; this was just one of countless occasions when he had tried to figure out whether he was being included in or excluded from something because of his race. What Lewis didn't understand was what to do. So he took a sheet of paper, drew a line down the middle, and began listing pros and cons.

The pros came quickly. "Opportunity" was the first thing Lewis wrote. At the end of his first week on the job, a fourth-year associate had told him, "The company is interested in making money. Either you're on the team producing, or you're not. That's it." By picking up the phone and saying yes to the trip, Lewis would show he was a team player.

Opportunity also meant something else to Lewis. Both his parents had been strong supporters of civil rights, and his mother was a well-known local activist in Seattle. During the early 1970s, she had spent two years suing her employer for discriminatory promotion practices. The lawsuit had been bitter and costly, but she had won. Lewis wondered if the St. Louis trip wasn't an opportunity to walk through the door his mother had helped pry open.

Lewis also wrote "Andy" on the list of pros. This was the heading for another set of considerations. Although Andy had volunteered to change his schedule, Lewis knew that he could make Andy's life a lot easier by going to St. Louis. Lewis had met Andy two years earlier—he was part of the recruiting team that had visited Lewis's MBA program. Since then, Andy had given Lewis a lot of advice, and Lewis liked the way he thought about things.

Lewis also realized that Andy was one of many people at the firm who had helped him out during the past year. The firm had treated him well, given him worthwhile assignments, and taught him more about business than he thought anyone could learn in a year. In addition, the firm paid him a salary that was much more than either of his parents earned.

Lewis next wrote down "Capitalism," thinking back on how his MBA finance professor would have viewed the situation. By attending the presentation, he would have said, Lewis would serve the interests of the firm and its shareholders, as its senior managers defined those interests. This obligation ended at the point of illegal or unethical behavior, but Lewis wasn't being asked to do anything illegal. Attending the presentation did involve dissembling, because Lewis had contributed nothing to the project, yet Andy seemed to indicate that this sort of bluffing was within the rules of the game in the industry. Moreover, by sending Lewis, the firm was trying to serve the client's interests, as the client defined them.

As Lewis reviewed the list of pros, he realized that most of his MBA classmates would have called the problem a "no-brainer." He looked at the phone and thought for a moment about calling to say yes to the trip, but decided to finish his analysis.

The first thing he wrote on the list of negatives was "Phony." Lewis was raised to tell the truth; one of his mother's favorite sayings was "The truth first." As a devout Christian, he believed that the Golden Rule demanded honesty in his dealings with others. How, then, could he go to St. Louis and pretend to be a member of the deal team? This could be called "bluffing," but that might be just a nice word for lying.

The next heading—"Malcolm"—made Lewis more uneasy. He was referring to Malcolm X—in particular, to a comment that an acquaintance had apparently made when he heard that Lewis had taken a job in investment banking. Lewis hadn't actually heard the comment (a friend passed it along), but it referred to Malcolm X's condemnation of "house slaves." They worked comfortably indoors, in return for telling their owners that they were fine and righteous masters—unlike the "field slaves," who had to toil under the hot sun, but with more of their dignity intact.

Lewis hadn't forgotten this comment. He believed in changing the system from within, and he liked Andy's idea that you had to play the game before you could make the rules. But he also understood discrimination. His parents had been its victims for much of their lives. Although Lewis had for the most part been spared overt discrimination, he vividly remembered being called a "watermelon picker" by players on an opposing grade school baseball team.

Now his firm was singling him out solely for his skin color, not for his talent. Lewis believed companies and clients should base decisions on performance, competence, and character, not on games of mix and match based on race, gender, and religion. Was including him as a token black really all that different from excluding him because he was black? What if a customer indicated that he would rather not have Jews or Asians working on a project? What if his firm could close more deals by ornamenting its presentations with pretty young women?

In the midst of these thoughts, Lewis looked at his watch; 45 minutes had passed. He had forgotten about his list of pros and cons, he was 10 minutes late for a meeting, and he still hadn't made a decision. Lewis quickly pulled out the folders he needed for the meeting and then slammed his desk drawer shut. Why was the St. Louis trip such a big deal? Did he have to think about everything as an African American? Couldn't he simply do his job, like any other young manager who wanted a successful career doing work he liked?

Steve Lewis's case illustrates the first basic type of right-versus-right problem: an urgent, complicated, and sometimes painful issue of personal integrity and moral identity. These are problems that raise the questions Who am I? and What is my moral center?

Notice that, as Steve Lewis struggled with his problem, he defined himself in several different ways. At different points in his thinking, he viewed himself as Andy's friend and protégé, as an employee and agent of his firm's shareholders, as a loyal and ambitious young investment banker, and as the son of parents whom he wanted to emulate. At some points, he was thinking of himself simply as a person; at others, as a Christian or an African American. None of these was the right way or the only way for Lewis to think about himself. But each entailed, in his mind, particular loyalties and obligations. Each answer to the question Who am I? sketched a particular way for Lewis to make decisions and live his life. Unfortunately, some answers suggested that Lewis should say yes to the trip; others required the answer no.

Lewis found his decision so difficult because he sensed, quite accurately, that it involved much more than the trip. It touched on the matter of who he was, what he stood for, and what regrets he would be willing to live with.

The challenge for Lewis, and for others facing questions like this, is not summoning the courage to do the right thing. The challenge is deciding *which right thing to do*. Lewis has to choose between right and right, on a complex issue of personal integrity. His question was not *whether* to be ethical; it was *how* to be ethical. His problem was the centrifugal pull of responsibilities to his employer, to its shareholders, to friends and his mentor, to himself, to his parents, and to his ideals.

It is tempting to dismiss Lewis's dilemma as a special case or a minor episode. Perhaps problems like this are restricted to beneficiaries of affirmative action programs. Perhaps investment banks are especially prone to ethical shenanigans. Perhaps the problem is mostly in Lewis's head, so that what he really needs to do is just make up his mind. Business calls for decisiveness; maybe Lewis should stop stewing in his own juice. And, in practical terms, the consequences of his decision are small: if Lewis doesn't go to St. Louis, Webster will.

Comments like these miss the essence of Lewis's problem. Experiences like Lewis's shape how people view their careers and themselves. Most managers can look back on a few early-career events that had far-reaching effects on their view of themselves and their sense of how the world works. These experiences are etched in their memory. They can recall mental pictures of key episodes, they still see how others' faces looked, and they feel again—often in the pit of their stomach—what they felt years earlier.

An acute sense of vulnerability and uncertainty often intensifies such recollections. As a young manager, Lewis is just beginning his effort to climb what British Prime Minister Benjamin Disraeli called "the greasy pole." Lewis was now playing in the big leagues and just learning the rules of the game, and he didn't want to make a naive mistake.

In this type of right-versus-right dilemma, it is crucial to look beyond the immediate practical consequences of a decision and examine how a decision can shape managers' views of obligations, their work, and their lives. Managers in these situations are like jugglers who are afraid to drop any of the balls they have in the air. Each is a part of themselves. Dropping one means failure, self-betrayal, feelings of regret and guilt—in a phrase, dirty hands. A later chapter will return to Lewis's dilemma, examine the way he resolved it, and assess these personal considerations in more detail.

MANAGERS IN THE MIDDLE

Conflicts of moral identity and personal integrity usually appear in sharpest relief in the early years of managers' careers. This is because organizations typically limit what apprentice managers can do and how much mischief they can make. As a result, the personal stakes in early-career dilemmas often outweigh the consequences for other people.*

For many managers, the balance soon shifts. Their careers prosper, and they find themselves in charge of a department, a branch, or some other business unit. Their decisions now affect the paychecks, self-respect, career opportunities, and families of other people—in short, their livelihoods and their lives. As a result, these managers often face problems less like Steve Lewis's and more like those of the veteran political leader in *Dirty Hands*. As the head of a unit of the Communist party, he was, roughly speaking, a middle manager in a large organization, with significant power over other people. With such power come serious responsibilities. When these responsibilities conflict with each other or with important personal values, managers face the second basic type of right-versus-right conflict.

A classic example of this kind of problem involved a 35-year-old manager, Peter Adario. Adario headed the marketing department of Sayer MicroWorld, a distributor of computer products. He was married and had three children. He had spent most of his career as a successful salesman and branch manager, and he eagerly accepted his present position because of its management challenges. Three senior managers reporting to Adario supervised the other 50 people in the marketing department. Adario reported to one of four vice presidents at corporate headquarters.

---

* There are surely exceptions to this generalization. The most notorious in recent years have been the so-called rogue traders, such as Nick Leeson at Baring Securities, who lost more than $1 billion and bankrupted his firm, or Joseph Jett, who was accused of creating phony bond trading profits, fatally weakening Kidder Peabody. But these exceptions are only partial. Closer examination of some of these cases indicates that the young managers did not act entirely on their own, but rather were given leeway and encouragement by their superiors.

Adario's dilemma arose from a conflict between Lisa Walters, one of the three senior managers who reported to him, and Kathryn McNeil, who worked for Lisa Walters. Walters wanted the company to fire McNeil. Adario had to decide whether to do so.

McNeil, 37 years old, had worked for Sayer MicroWorld for only four months. She was the IBM product manager, a job for which she seemed well suited because she had worked in marketing at IBM for eight years. McNeil was responsible for Sayer's purchases of personal computers from IBM. She and her two assistants handled $40 million of products each month. Their work involved daily contact with IBM, negotiation of pricing and delivery dates for the retailers, constant communication with the Sayer reps who sold IBM products at the retail stores, announcements of problems or product changes, and weekly analyses of the IBM product line for corporate headquarters.

McNeil worked for Lisa Walters, a single woman in her late twenties. Walters handled the IBM account during the two years before McNeil was hired, and she excelled at the job, consistently meeting deadlines and demonstrating initiative in promoting her product line.

Lisa Walters worked longer hours than most of her colleagues, never taking lunch breaks and seldom leaving the office before 8:00 P.M. She had a serious, down-to-business personality that impressed and, on occasion, irritated Adario. Nevertheless, he respected Walters's high professional standards and knew he could count on her, no matter how demanding the circumstances. Two years earlier, when one of the senior manager positions opened up, Adario immediately recommended Walters for the post. Her work since then had been excellent.

Walters wanted to fire McNeil because McNeil's work was falling behind schedule. McNeil was a devoted mother with full custody of her six-year-old and no child support or other assistance from her ex-husband. Walters believed that McNeil's responsibilities at home were causing her problems at work. Walters had grown frustrated and very impatient with the situation.

Adario believed that the conflict between Walters and McNeil had been intensified by the hothouse atmosphere in which everyone was working. Computer retailing was a low-margin, highly competitive business. Sayer's strategy depended heavily on completing a merger with a recently acquired competitor and paying down the debt that financed the deal. Under these pressures, 10- to 12-hour days had become common. Because most of the employees in Adario's department were in their twenties and unmarried, the long hours hadn't raised work-family issues.

Adario had not paid much attention to Walters's concerns until the morning he found a handwritten note from her on top of his pile of unfinished paperwork. It was her second note in as many weeks. Both complained about McNeil's hours, and both mentioned replacing her. Adario realized that the conflict between Walters and McNeil wouldn't end unless he got involved. He would have acted sooner but had hesitated because he was pulled in two different directions.

On one hand, although McNeil was working 60 hours a week, she was not pulling her weight. Everyone else, including Adario, was working longer hours. Moreover, no letup was in sight—because of the merger, the debt load, and the nature of the computer retailing business. McNeil's work on the all-important IBM account was clearly behind schedule, and her relationship with Walters had deteriorated badly. When Adario thought about the work that lay ahead, he felt that Walters's suggestion was close to the mark. He was inclined to find a replacement for McNeil and then let her go.

At the same time, however, Adario had a serious reservation about this approach. On several occasions, Sayer's executives had said they believed in creating a "family-friendly" workplace, and a headquarters task force was studying ways to do this. Adario viewed the Kathryn McNeil situation as an opportunity to do something tangible along these lines. He didn't think of himself as a crusader or reformer, but he believed that people worked better when the rest of their lives were sane.

This professional conviction was reinforced by Adario's personal experiences. Like McNeil, he was barely seeing his own family. And his wife had given up her job as an accountant when their second child was born after struggling with inflexible work schedules at two different employers. In addition, Adario's next-door neighbor had been laid off three years earlier, when his company had restructured; even though he soon found another job, his self-esteem and confidence had been badly damaged. Above all, Adario thought it was simply wrong to fire someone, especially a dedicated single parent, who was working very hard at her job.

What is distinctive about Peter Adario's right-versus-right conflict? If we compare his problem to Steve Lewis's, the answer becomes clear. One important difference has already been noted: the scope of a manager's power and responsibility. Lewis's primary responsibilities were *to* others and *to* himself. Managers like Adario are also responsible *for* other people.

In addition, Steve Lewis's problem raised fundamental personal questions, such as Who am I? and What do I stand for? In contrast, Peter Adario's decision raised basic organizational questions: Who are we? What do we stand for? What norms and values guide how we work together and treat each other? How do we define ourselves as a human institution?

These organizational questions do not replace the issues of moral identity and personal integrity that Steve Lewis faced. In reality, they are closely intertwined with them. If Adario supports Walter's recommendation to fire McNeil, he will be making a personal commitment to a particular set of values: serving the interests of Sayer's shareholders and customers, protecting the jobs of people in the company, and defining fairness as expecting the same effort from everyone on a team. But, if he supports Walters's recommendation, Adario will weaken or even disavow his personal and professional commitments to vulnerable people like McNeil and her son, as he does to them what other bosses did to his wife and his neighbor.

But Adario's decision cannot remain purely personal. Its consequences will ripple far and wide. The people working for him will watch carefully and interpret his decision—to understand what his values are, how much they can trust him, and how they have to behave if they want to get ahead. Adario's choice will shape the rules of the game and define what fairness means in the small human community he leads. Does fairness mean that everyone pulls an equal weight? Or does it mean that managers should take account of the legitimate personal needs of their dedicated employees?

Adario and managers like him are truly "managers in the middle."[1] They are pulled in different directions by their bosses, peers, and subordinates, and by their personal values and commitments. Often they bear the burden of difficult decisions even though they have "a boss's responsibility without a boss's authority." Most are under intense pressure to deliver the profits their company's executives have promised to shareholders. Restructuring and reengineering threaten their jobs.

These pressures also distinguish their right-versus-right conflicts from early-career issues like Steve Lewis's. Young managers are sometimes advised to put aside six months' salary as "go to hell" money. In theory, these funds enable them to quit a bad job and spend time finding a good one. But things are more complicated for managers like Adario, because they are "in the middle" in yet another sense. These men and women are often well along life's path—with families, mortgages, professional relationships, and expertise in particular kinds of work. Rarely can they tell their bosses where to go and storm out the door. They usually have little choice, at least in the short run, but to soldier onward, no matter how difficult the circumstances.

Right-versus-right decisions *force* managers in the middle to make choices. When we return to Peter Adario's problem in a later chapter, we will see that he had no option labeled "Do nothing" or "Quit the job." He must choose—and in doing so commit himself and his department. It was right-versus-right conflicts like these that led Chester Barnard to warn about the moral destruction that sometimes threatens managers and to admire deeply the men and women who find practical, responsible ways to resolve these conflicts.

NEGOTIATED ETHICS

The third type of right-versus-right conflict is the most complex and challenging. In these cases, managers have personal responsibilities *to* themselves and *to* other groups, as did Steve Lewis. Like Peter Adario, they are responsible *for* others, sometimes for an entire organization. But this third kind of right-versus-right problem involves responsibilities that a company shares *with* other groups in society.

A classic definition of a company describes it as an independent economic unit or, more elegantly, as "an island of managerial control in a sea of market relations."[2] This view, however, is badly out of date and appears only in introductory economics books. In reality, most firms are now enmeshed in networks of ongoing relationships. Strategic alliances link firms with their customers and suppliers, and sometimes with labor unions, governments, university laboratories, and even competitors. Many companies also have complicated dealings with the media, government regulators, local communities, and various interest groups.

These networks of relationships are also networks of managerial responsibility. Taken together, a company's business partners and stakeholders have a wide range of legitimate claims, but no company can satisfy all of them. Obligations to some groups often collide with those to others. At times, these stakeholder responsibilities conflict with managers' personal and organizational obligations. When these conflicts occur, managers confront the third type of right-versus-right problem.

A dramatic example of this type of conflict has been unfolding in the pharmaceutical industry since 1988. Late that year, the senior management of Roussel-Uclaf, a medium-sized French pharmaceutical company with less than $2 billion in annual sales, had to decide where and how to market a new drug, called RU 486. Early tests had shown that the drug was 90 to 95 percent effective in causing miscarriage during the first five weeks of pregnancy. The drug came to be known as "the French abortion pill," and Roussel-Uclaf and its managers found themselves at the vortex of the abortion controversy.

The chairman of Roussel-Uclaf, Edouard Sakiz, was a physician with a longstanding personal commitment to RU 486. He would make the final decisions on introducing the drug. Earlier in his career, while working as a medical researcher, Sakiz had helped develop the chemical compound on which RU 486 was based. He believed strongly that the drug could help thousands of women, particularly in poor countries, avoid injury or death from botched abortions. In the developed world, he believed, RU 486 would provide women and physicians with a valuable alternative to surgical abortions.

But Sakiz couldn't base his decisions on RU 486 solely on his personal values. As the head of a company, he had other important obligations. Some were to his shareholders; from this perspective, RU 486 was a serious problem. Revenues from the drug were likely to be quite small, particularly in the early years. Yet, during this period, antiabortion groups would mount an international boycott of products made by Roussel-Uclaf and Hoechst, the German chemical giant that was Roussel-Uclaf's largest shareholder. A successful boycott would cost the two companies far more than they would earn from RU 486. At worst, a boycott could imperil Roussel-Uclaf's survival, for it was a relatively small company with weak profits.

Like any executive, Sakiz also had responsibilities *for* the people in his firm. He had to assess the seriousness of the threats of violence against Roussel-Uclaf and its employees. At the same time, Sakiz's decisions about RU 486 would define the fundamental values of Roussel Uclaf. This was an especially important issue because his employees were sharply divided about the drug. Some were passionately committed to RU 486, while others opposed the drug on ethical grounds or feared that the protests and boycotts would harm Roussel-Uclaf and its other products. Sakiz knew that debates about the product and the company's responsibilities were sapping employee morale and diverting a good deal of management time. He also knew that his decisions would commit Roussel-Uclaf to one stand or another.

Thus, at a personal level, Sakiz faced a version of the question Who am I? Was he, first and foremost, a medical doctor, a scientific researcher, an advocate of women's rights, or a corporate executive with responsibilities to shareholders and employees? In addition, his decisions on RU 486 would commit his company to some values rather than others, thereby answering the organizational question Who are we?

Personal and organizational issues like those facing Sakiz are difficult enough. But the prospect of introducing RU 486 placed him at the center of a network of responsibilities to important groups and institutions outside Roussel-Uclaf. One of these was the French government. It owned 36 percent of Roussel-Uclaf, and the French Ministry of Health closely regulated the company, thus shaping its business opportunities. The French government supported the introduction of RU 486 on the basis of women's rights, the value of a less invasive medical procedure, and the prospect of lowering the nation's health care costs by substituting a pill for surgery.

Hoechst, which owned 55 percent of Roussel-Uclaf, was another critical stakeholder, and it, too, made strong ethical claims on Roussel-Uclaf. Its chairman was a devout Roman Catholic, who opposed abortion on moral grounds and had repeatedly stated his position in public. Moreover, Hoechst had a mission statement committing the firm to lofty goals, which was put in place partly in reaction to Hoechst's role in producing Zyklon B, a poison gas used in the gas chambers at Auschwitz. (This bit of history was not lost on antiabortion protesters; some marched outside Roussel-Uclaf's offices, carrying posters that read "RU 486 turns a woman's uterus into a death chamber.")

China was another powerful actor in the drama. It wanted access to RU 486 for population control. The moral ground for China's position was avoiding the misery and risks of starvation resulting from its surging population.

Roussel-Uclaf's network of relationships and responsibilities raised extremely difficult questions for Sakiz and Roussel-Uclaf. What, in fact, were the company's obligations to women? To the government laboratory that helped develop the steroid molecule on which RU 486 was based? To the larger medical and research communities? Were the unborn a stakeholder group? Could Roussel-Uclaf introduce the drug both in the West, citing a woman's right to choose, and in China, where women had apparently been coerced into abortions, even near the end of their pregnancies?

In later chapters, we will return to Sakiz's exceedingly complex problem. For now, it is important to notice how it compares to the problems facing Steve Lewis and Peter Adario. In one respect, Sakiz's situation clearly parallels theirs. He had to make a decision that involved, in direct and powerful ways, his personal integrity and moral identity. In Sakiz's case, these personal issues involved the morality of abortion and his responsibilities as a human being, an executive, and a physician and medical researcher. Sakiz's decision also resembles Peter Adario's: in both cases, their decisions will define important values for their organizations.

But Sakiz's situation differs from the other two in a crucial way. His decisions on RU 486 will define his firm's role in society and its relationships with its stakeholders. These powerful groups and important institutions were pushing and pulling the company in different directions. Each of them had staked out a clear moral position on RU 486. Some wanted Roussel-Uclaf to abandon RU

486. Others wanted it available, as soon as possible, around the world. Still others advocated a gradual introduction, starting only in developed countries, which had the medical infrastructure to deal with any unexpected side effects from the new drug.

There was no way for Sakiz to satisfy all these claims. As in the other two cases, right collided with right. Unlike those cases, however, the RU 486 issue involved a wide range of responsibilities and relationships outside Sakiz's firm. As a result, this type of right-versus-right problem has a distinctive feature: a company and its managers cannot resolve these problems unilaterally.

When power over a decision is shared and fragmented, an extensive period of jockeying, maneuvering, and sometimes attack and counterattack precedes and shapes the final resolution of this type of right-versus-right issue. As a result, a company's responsibilities, its role in society, and its relations with stakeholders do not, and cannot, spring full-blown from the internal deliberations of its managers. They are inevitably negotiated with stakeholders. This task usually falls to a company's senior executives, as it did in the RU 486 case.

The difficulty of this task can be concealed by benign words like *negotiation, stakeholders,* and *strategic ally.* In reality, managers sometimes must bargain with and battle against powerful adversarial groups: some of a company's stakeholders—such as the antiabortion groups in the RU 486 case—want to drive a stake through the heart of its plans. This raises a whole new set of issues, both managerial and ethical. When, for example, should managers fight fire with fire? And what are the most effective and responsible ways to do so?

The complexity of right-versus-right problems escalates to its highest level with problems like RU 486. These situations are the managerial equivalent of the game of three-dimensional chess. Ordinary chess is difficult enough, but this game is played on three chessboards, stacked one above the other. Players can move and capture on any board, so that whatever happens on one board inevitably affects the other two. Managers face similar complexity when a right-versus-right issue involves their personal, organizational, and societal responsibilities.

Thus Sakiz's problem is the most complex version of the conflict that Steve Lewis and Peter Adario faced. In all three cases, some of a manager's responsibilities conflicted with others. The stakes were high, and there was no exit—a manager had to decide, choose, commit, and act. Doing one right thing would sacrifice others. Each situation confirmed the view of Sartre's veteran political leader: dirty hands situations are sometimes the inescapable lot of men and women with real responsibilities in life.

But perhaps Sartre is too gloomy. Perhaps these problems aren't really so grave. It may be possible to find what Oliver Wendell Holmes sought—"the simplicity on the other side of complexity"—if only one looks in the right places. Perhaps managers can rely on fundamental ethical principles, or the law, or carefully crafted company mission statements and ethical guidelines, to clear a path through these ethical conflicts. Or perhaps managers should simply consult their moral instincts and intuitions, and then pursue a course of action that they can live with in good conscience.

3

↔

The Futility of Grand Principles

ECALL THE QUESTION Steve Lewis asked after slamming his desk drawer shut: Why was the St. Louis trip such a big deal? Like almost everyone, Lewis had been brought up to know the difference between right and wrong, and he desperately wanted to do the right thing. So what was the problem? Why was he so frustrated?

At least three sources of moral guidance were available to Steve Lewis, Peter Adario, and Edouard Sakiz. These were the mission statements and ethical guidelines of their companies, their legal responsibilities, and the fundamental principles of traditional moral philosophy.

Sakiz, for example, could have turned to his own company, Roussel-Uclaf, and to its partner Hoechst for guidance on the RU 486 decision. Both had statements of their corporate missions and values. Because issues of social responsibility are particularly important for drug companies and chemical companies, Sakiz could reasonably expect these documents to help him make his decision.

And suppose that Peter Adario had asked an attorney what legal principles he should follow in making his decision about Kathryn McNeil. In all likelihood, a lawyer would have reminded him of managers' duty to serve their shareholders' interests and, in basic terms, of the laws on discrimination and employees' rights. Surely this advice would provide sound criteria for Peter's decision.

Finally, suppose that Steve Lewis had studied philosophy in college. He would have learned about John Stuart Mill and Immanuel Kant. These men, two of the most powerful intellects of modern times, developed two of the best-known theories of ethics. Mill, the nineteenth-century British philosopher and social reformer, believed there was an objective, universal principle for resolving ethical issues. In simple terms, this principle was choosing the course of action that brought the greatest happiness to the greatest number of people.*

Kant was an eighteenth-century German philosopher. He believed that actions were morally correct if they conformed to the moral law and if the person performing the actions intended to do his or her duty. In Steve Lewis's case, such duties would include telling the truth, keeping promises, and respecting others' rights. Hence, Kant's advice to Lewis would be to do his duty, and Mill's would be to do the greatest good for the greatest number.

All these principles—corporate, legal, and philosophical—require careful examination. But even this brief introduction indicates why they are so appealing to people who must make difficult practical decisions: general principles seem to offer clear, straightforward ways to solve difficult problems.

Unfortunately, however, they provide little aid or comfort when managers face right-versus-right dilemmas. The grand principles are too general and tend to float above problems. They often contradict each other, tightening the Gordian knot rather than cutting through it. And, most importantly, the decisive factors in

---

* Interpretations vary, but a common view among philosophers is that Mill was a rule-utilitarian rather than an act-utilitarian. That is, he believed that the basic principle of maximizing happiness provided the justification of middle-level rights, duties, and other ethical rules. These rules, in turn, could be used for guidance on particular actions. In contrast, an act-utilitarian skips middle-level rules and judges each action by its consequences for the sum total of happiness.

right-versus-right situations are practical and personal. One must be immersed in a situation, and one must know who one is, in order to determine the right thing to do.

The best way to understand why grand principles provide little guidance for right-versus-right situations is to examine the grand principles closely and assess their value for managers facing the kinds of problems that Lewis, Adario, and Sakiz confronted.

CREDOS AND MISSION STATEMENTS

In the last two decades, many companies have introduced mission statements, credos, and similar guides to responsible decision making. Mission statements typically invoke high principles and dedicate a firm to some broader social mission. Steve Jobs, for example, described the mission of Apple Computer as "contributing to this world by making tools for the mind that advance mankind." Often companies translate fundamental commitments like this into more specific terms, by writing company credos and codes of conduct.[1]

The corporate credo of Johnson & Johnson, the pharmaceutical company, is widely known and respected. It says the firm has four responsibilities. The first is to "doctors, nurses, and patients, to mothers and fathers, and all others who use our products and services." The credo fleshes out this commitment in terms of high quality, cost control, and other factors. The firm's other responsibilities are, in order of importance, to its employees, to the communities in which it does business, and to its stockholders, who are promised a "fair return."

What would Edouard Sakiz have learned if he consulted the two corporate credos available to him at the time of the RU 486 decision? Imagine looking over his shoulder as he searches these statements for guidance.

Like others of its kind, the Hoechst credo describes the company's basic objectives and values. The company would, for example, be "the recognized leader in its target markets." But were abortion-related products a target market? Hoechst's mission statement said its management aimed "to continuously increase the long-term value of the company." This suggests shelving the product, given that boycotts against RU 486 would likely hurt profits. But the mission statement also committed the company to developing products that would "meet people's basic needs and improve the quality of life while safeguarding and raising living standards." This worthy objective, which is phrased quite generally, can easily be read as an endorsement of RU 486.

Given these ambiguities, a crucial issue was who had the authority to make the RU 486 decision. To this question, the mission statement gave the Delphic answer, "We operate in a decentralized manner, allowing each business to develop within our values." What were these values? At this point, Sakiz would be ensnared in a catch-22. Perhaps he needed to return to the beginning of the mission statement and try to do a more careful job of interpreting the values it salutes?

Roussel-Uclaf also had a corporate credo. Unfortunately, it was even more vexing than Hoechst's. The statement committed Roussel-Uclaf to many high-minded goals: a spirit of cooperation, creativity, a spirit of achievement, forward planning, and adaptation to major scientific, technological, and social changes. These goals were unproblematic, but another set off loud, flashing alarms on the RU 486 decision. The company had committed itself to "placing our energy, our ideas, and our dedication in the service of Life."

One problem with this goal is obvious: its near-vacuity. What, if anything, does "Life" mean when used in this exceedingly general way? Is the company making clear that it is not dedicated to "Death"? The other problem is far more serious. What does "Life" mean in the context of the abortion debate? Does it refer to the life of the mother or the fetus or the unborn? A broad affirmation of life is of little value in the search for practical guidance on RU 486.

These difficulties reflect the two fundamental problems of relying on corporate credos and mission statements to resolve right-versus-right conflicts. One problem is that these statements are too vague. For example, one business school professor regularly asked groups of managers to write down their company's mission statement. Then he put their notes in a shoebox, picked one at random, and asked whose credo it was. "Inevitably," he reported, "five or six hands would go up, as managers from airlines, pharmaceutical companies, and plumbing supply manufacturers all claimed the statement as their own."[2]

There are many reasons for the vagueness problem. Most credos and mission statements, like those at Roussel-Uclaf and Hoechst, are quite short yet must cover a multitude of situations. They cannot provide much guidance for countless varied, complex situations. No brief statement could.

In other cases, mission statements are vague because companies have put them together with little thought and use them for public relations or for hits of inspiration at company gatherings. They are the rough equivalent of playing the national anthem before a sporting event. At best, these feckless efforts deserve the epitaph that American writer H. L. Mencken suggested for Calvin Coolidge: "He did no harm and was not a nuisance." More typically, the purely inspirational approach breeds cynicism, as employees recognize that their company credo is only a wall decoration for executive offices.

But even good intentions and serious effort cannot overcome the vagueness problem. It affects even companies that take their ethics efforts seriously. The problem is that these statements try to simplify what is inescapably complex. Many credos, for example, endorse fairness. But what *is* fairness? Can it be pinned down in one or two carefully crafted phrases? A colleague of mine once asked a group of experienced managers to define fairness. By the end of a long and heated discussion, in which the managers referred to many of their own experiences, seven or eight different definitions of fairness emerged. These included playing by the rules of the game, following basic morality, treating everyone alike and not playing favorites, treating others as you would want to be treated, being sensitive to individuals' needs, providing equal opportunity for everyone, and creating a level playing field for the disadvantaged.

Each of these definitions captures an important aspect of fairness, and all make ethical sense, but they differ from each other in crucial ways. Fairness, like other basic human values, cannot be defined in a single phrase. This dooms credos to vacuity.[3]

Many thoughtful executives have tried to address the vagueness issue—60 percent of American companies now have detailed codes of conduct, designed to translate basic company values into specific terms. One-third of American firms have ethics training programs or ethics officers.[4] Many are now working with law firms and public accounting firms to make these programs as effective as possible. But even these comprehensive ethics programs are of little help with right-versus-right issues.

The problem is not vagueness, but the fact that these initiatives focus overwhelmingly on problems of misconduct and wrongdoing—stealing, taking bribes, sexual harassment, falsifying documents, and the like. In fact, many recent efforts are responses to the 1991 U.S. Federal Sentencing Guidelines for Organizations. These programs deal with right and wrong. But Steve Lewis, Peter Adario, and Edouard Sakiz were struggling with right-versus-right conflicts. None was contemplating an illegal act.

For them and for other managers facing serious conflicts of responsibility, the problem is defining what fairness, "Life," and other basic values mean—but not in a few inspiring words engraved on a company paperweight or poster. These managers need definitions-in-action—concrete ways of resolving messy, ambiguous problems, under relentless pressures of time, budgets, and uncertainty. From their perspective, credos and mission statements seem to be products of what American philosopher and psychologist William James called the "world of the philosophy-professor," a realm that is "simple, noble, and clean. The contradictions of real life are absent from it. Its architecture is classic. . . . Purity and dignity are what it most expresses. It is a kind of marble temple shining on a hill."[5]

In most cases, credos, mission statements, and ethics programs are crafted with care. They express genuine and admirable sentiments. They can help managers understand right and wrong in the context of their business. But, for a manager facing a right-versus-right issue, credos and mission statements are often the rough equivalent of someone standing on a pier and offering three feet of magnificently braided rope to a person struggling in the water 20 feet below.

LEGAL DUTIES

Perhaps the answer is to avoid loading too much responsibility onto credos and mission statements, to dig deeper and seek firmer guidance for the ethical issues of everyday management.

Business law is a natural alternative. The law, of course, is far more than a set of rules and punishments. In a democracy, it expresses the political and moral judgments of society. Corporate law, in the Anglo-American tradition, has evolved over centuries, through myriad case decisions, scores of important pieces of legislation, and high court interpretations of fundamental principles. This makes business law quite promising for our purposes. It presents a clear ethical obligation for business managers: performing their basic legal duties.

And what are these? Here, once again, a clear, firm answer seems readily available. The most famous recent statement of these duties appeared in a 1970 article in the *New York Times Magazine*. Its title summarized its basic theme: "The Social Responsibility of Business Is to Increase Its Profits." In the article, its author, Nobel laureate economist Milton Friedman, wrote:

> *In a free-enterprise, private-property system, a corporate executive is an employee of the owners of the business. He has direct responsibility to his employers. That responsibility is to conduct the business in accordance with their desires, which generally will be to make as much money as possible while conforming to the basic rules of society, both those embodied in law and those embodied in ethical custom.*[6]

This definition of managers' duties seems to give clear marching orders to someone like Peter Adario. In deciding whether to replace Kathryn McNeil, his basic objectives should be to follow the law and to contribute to his company's profits. At first glance, this principle seems to offer clear, tangible, perhaps even quantifiable standards. Unfortunately, as with many first glances, this one deceives.

Under the law on employment and discrimination, it was perfectly legal for Adario to fire Kathryn McNeil. When Kathryn McNeil accepted her job at Sayer MicroWorld, she signed an employment contract with a standard employee-at-will provision, stating that "either you or the company is free to terminate the employment relationship at any time for any reason." The only exception to this provision involved so-called public policy issues: an employee could not be fired, for example, if he or she missed work for jury duty. However, no public policy exemptions applied in Kathryn McNeil's situation. In short, the law told Adario he could fire McNeil but gave him no guidance on whether to do so.

The grand principle of capitalism that Friedman cites also lets Adario down: it was simply too general to provide practical guidance. To understand this, assume that he accepts the principle as gospel truth and vows to maximize profits. Notice how little this helps him with the issues he must resolve. Obviously, a replacement who worked longer hours than McNeil and did the same caliber of work would add to profits. But to what extent would this gain be offset by the costs and delays of finding and training a replacement, and by any severance pay McNeil receives? Morale and productivity would likely improve, at least in the short run, because grumbling about McNeil's special treatment would cease. But by how much? And how costly would the continuation of Sayer's high-intensity, "churn-and-burn" personnel practices be in the long run? What are the costs of limiting the company's labor pool by discouraging talented people like Kathryn McNeil from seeking jobs at Sayer? How much would a family-friendly approach contribute to profits? Will Sayer be there for the long run if it doesn't keep sprinting in the short run?

These are just some of the many practical issues Adario would face as he tried to determine how firing Kathryn McNeil would affect his department's profits. The decisive considerations for Adario were practical, local, and specific to his situation. Invoking the grand principle of maximizing profits adds little. Adario, like everyone else at Sayer MicroWorld, already knew that profits mattered critically.

The problem with the grand principles of capitalism actually runs even deeper. "Maximize profits for shareholders" is no more than an extraordinarily simplistic mantra. It does little justice to the rich tradition of laws and ideas that gave birth to modern capitalism. If Adario searches these ideas for guidance, he will come away enlightened. But he will also be confused and may well get contradictory advice about what he should do.

For decades, an important debate has engaged lawyers, economists, philosophers, and thoughtful business managers. Its basic issue was summarized in another astutely crafted title, this one written by E. Merrick Dodd in a classic *Harvard Law Review* article. The title he chose was the ostensibly simple question: "For Whom Are Corporate Managers Trustees?"[7] What is remarkable about Dodd's article is that it was written more than half a century ago, in 1932, yet the issues it raised remain in sharp dispute. The terms are different now. As Dodd phrased the issue, managers were trustees who had social service as well as profit-making obligations. Today, the question is whether managers are responsible to shareholders or to all of their stakeholders.

This is no ivory tower dispute. It arises in takeover battles, during layoffs, and in decisions about opening plants overseas. By the early 1990s, 29 states had passed so-called corporate constituency laws, permitting companies to consider nonshareholder interests when they make major decisions.

What is the upshot of these issues for a manager like Peter Adario? If Adario accepts the *shareholder* view, his duty is to earn the highest profits he can for Sayer MicroWorld's owners. This may well mean firing Kathryn McNeil. If he accepts the *stakeholder* view, he must take account of McNeil's welfare and perhaps even her son's. This may mean reducing profits to save her job.

Efforts to describe how managers should balance the interests of competing stakeholder groups have thus far yielded unhelpful generalities. For example, a distinguished group of experienced attorneys, working under the aegis of the American Law Institute, recently published an account of the objectives of the corporation. It stated that the basic objective was "enhancing corporate profit and shareholder gain." This sounds plain and clear. But several pages of the report interpret, qualify, and hedge this prescription, almost into oblivion. Managers, for example, are encouraged to take ethical considerations into account, as long as these are "reasonably regarded as appropriate to the responsible conduct of the business."[8] But what is *reasonable?* What is *responsible?* These words are as general and unhelpful as *fairness.*

Answers to hard questions like these become clear only from a vantage point far removed from the everyday pressures and challenges of managers' work. Indeed, they attain crystalline clarity in the minds of academic economists, such as Milton Friedman, whose management experience usually involves little more than supervising a secretary or a research team. Ironically, these economists typically have or aspire to lifetime tenure, which liberates them from the market pressures they advocate for managers like Peter Adario and for the rest of humanity as well.

Most executives reject simplistic answers. A recent study found that a clear majority of American executives defined their basic responsibility as preserving the long-term health and vitality of their companies, while meeting obligations to a range of stakeholders. However, these executives had no formula for balancing their multiple obligations.[9] And if they look to the courts for help, they will find judges interpreting the newly minted corporate constituency laws, a process that will last for years. What the nonshareholder interests are, and when and how they should be considered, remains a matter of intepretation and dispute.[10]

In short, if Peter Adario consults the grand principles of capitalism in a serious way, he will learn only one thing with full certainty: the debate about managers' fundamental legal and ethical duties is far from over. The further Adario pursues a precise definition of his duties, the thicker the tangle in which he will find himself.

THE ETHICS MACHINE

Perhaps the answer is to dig even deeper—beyond corporate credos and legal duties—and look for some bedrock philosophical principles. Perhaps these could help managers interpret their companies' mission statements, trade off their obligations to various stakeholders, and resolve right-versus-right conflicts.

This approach has a long, distinguished genealogy. For centuries, philosophers, theologians, and other thinkers have aspired to find a fundamental, universal, objective standard for resolving difficult ethical issues. The contemporary philosopher Alasdair MacIntyre has called this effort the "Enlightenment project."[11] This was the dream, first conceived in Europe three centuries ago, of relying on reason to comprehend both human nature and the physical world.

In the sphere of ethics, the goal was also extremely ambitious. Philosophers sought to find an overarching, rational justification for morality—a set of basic principles that were independent of religion, tradition, culture, or individual beliefs. Some philosophers have described this endeavor as the quest to replace the biased, subjective, all-too-human approach to ethical issues with a transcendent, "God's-eye" perspective.[12]

If these philosophers had succeeded, the results would have been extraordinary. Once discovered, the fundamental ethical principle could serve as a morality machine. It could, in effect, be placed at the end of a conveyor belt, and people could feed their ethical problems into it. After a period of clanking and chugging, the machine would apply the fundamental principle to the problems and then give answers. For example, the fundamental ethical principle could help someone like Steve Lewis rank the various "right" things he felt obliged to do, and then he could learn whether he should go to the St. Louis presentation. Peter Adario could learn what to do about Lisa Walters and Kathryn McNeil. And Edouard Sakiz could learn the most responsible way to introduce RU 486.

The notion of a morality machine is, of course, a caricature. Few philosophers have believed that their principles should be applied to problems in rigid, mechanical ways. None claimed to have a universal tool for the problems of life. Yet the image of an ethics machine captures a basic feature of this approach to practical ethical issues: its goal of finding a universal, objective principle for resolving hard ethical problems.

The Enlightenment project failed to achieve this goal. What it produced, instead, were several different theories of ethics. Each claimed to be objective and universal—and each, in fundamental ways, contradicted the others. MacIntyre describes the dismaying consequences in these words: "The most striking feature of contemporary moral utterance is that so much of it is used to express disagreements; and the most striking feature of the debates in which these disagreements are expressed is their interminable character."[13] As a result, forays into the academic realm of competing ethical theories will provide little guidance to managers with right-versus-right dilemmas.

Consider one of the favorite puzzles of contemporary moral philosophers. Pedro walks into a village and finds Jim holding 20 people hostage. Jim says he will kill them all unless Pedro takes a gun and kills one of the hostages. All of the hostages are innocent people. What should Pedro do?

The basic principle of John Stuart Mill's utilitarian ethics is, in rough terms, to do whatever brings about the greatest good for the greatest number. This is the ethics of consequences. It points Pedro in the direction of killing 1 hostage; if he does so, 20 people will live.

The basic principle of Kant's deontological ethics—which, roughly speaking, demands that people do their moral duty—tells Pedro that his duty is to respect the right to life of an innocent person. The ethics of duty prohibits him from killing the single hostage. But then Jim will slaughter 20 innocent people.

In short, two of the most important grand principles of moral philosophy give contradictory answers to Pedro's urgent practical problem. True, they clarify the problems by cutting to the quick and revealing the basic ethical trade-off. But, at the same time, they intensify the problem, thereby tightening a Gordian knot by providing powerful, conflicting definitions of what is right. This problem is hardly confined to contrived cases like that of Jim and Pedro. In many right-versus-right dilemmas, the morality of consequences clashes with the morality of rights and duties. Perhaps the most momentous of these arose when President Harry S Truman decided to wage a nuclear war against Japan. In terms of consequences, the use of nuclear weapons may have ended the war more quickly, thereby saving the hundreds of thousands of Americans and Japanese who would have perished in a land invasion of Japan. At the same time, the bombs incinerated thousands of innocent infants and children, and scarred others for life. The ethics of consequences seems to justify Truman's decision. The violation of the rights of the innocent condemns it.

Philosophers are still at work on ethical theory. Some have adapted the insights of Mill and Kant and created new versions of their theories; others offer new principles for ethical decisions. Each school of philosophy believes it has knock-down arguments against its adversaries, but none has vanquished the others. The debates are quite complex and elicit brilliant intellectual fireworks, but they cast dim light on practical problems.*

Steve Lewis, for example, was trying to assess the ethical issues involved in going to St. Louis or avoiding the trip. Each alternative had different consequences for himself, his client, his firm, and for other African Americans who would follow after him. But he understood this. He also had to balance his own rights as a human being, as a member of a minority group, and as an employee against the rights of his firm and its clients. But Lewis also knew this. And, if fundamental principles contribute little to a "simple" right-versus-right issue like Lewis's, someone in a complex predicament, like Edouard Sakiz, should not expect much help from them.

The futility of these grand principles for right-versus-right problems will shock few thoughtful managers. They understand that fundamental values and responsibilities collide in some situations. They know that the solution to these problems is more than a matter of calling the local university and hiring a Kantian as a consultant.[14] Managers sense, quite correctly, that what philosophers have failed to resolve in theory they must somehow resolve in practice.

---

* Perhaps these thinkers are really playing their own fascinating, complex game—not the equivalent of Monopoly, but a form of deep play comparable to high-level chess. In fact, philosophers often refer to their arguments as "moves." Moreover, many arguments and counterarguments in specialized areas of professional ethics have become so familiar and stylized that someone will eventually codify them using chess notation. For example, P-K4: Market preferences have strong moral weight because they reflect the preferences of participants in markets. P-K4: But markets are often imperfect. N-KB3: Citizens can use the political process to regulate markets and deal with market failures; thus regulated markets have strong moral weight. N-QB3: But some market participants, like large corporations, have unfair influence on regulations, so markets remain distorted. A less-flattering view of these efforts has been proposed by a fellow philosopher, Richard Rorty, who has condemned "the neurotic quest for certainty" that underlies, in his view, a good deal of philosophical writing.

ETHICS AS AN ELECTRIFIED FENCE

Perhaps practical people should simply forget about the grand princi-ples. Mission statements can be left to the staff at headquarters, which will give them something to do. Economists and lawyers can wrangle over fiduciary duties, and philosophers can pursue the ethical superprinciple. Meanwhile, everyone else can get down to real work.

This strategy would be a serious mistake, for the grand principles serve vital purposes. First, they can clarify fundamental issues at stake in a practical problem. Mission statements and credos can remind managers of the larger purposes their work serves, something easily lost in the hurly-burly of everyday life. Moreover, the question of which stakeholders matter the most is critical to many manage-ment decisions.

Second, the grand philosophical principles are essential for under-standing the difference between right and wrong, between good and evil. They serve, in effect, as an electrified fence that separates a sphere of right actions from a surrounding territory of wrong ones. In this way, the basic principles of philosophy undergird the laws, rules, and social practices that make civilized life possible. The grand principles enable Steve Lewis to understand when his rights are being violated and to take action when this is the case. Without the grand principles, and without the institutions that translate them into practice, life would degenerate into what the political philoso-pher Thomas Hobbes called "the war of all against all."

Unfortunately, however, within the boundaries defined and de-fended by the grand principles, one right action sometimes conflicts with another. In these cases, the principles are too general, and they are sometimes contradictory. In addition, managers must make their decisions from the ground up, not downward from a realm of theory. Hence, mission statements, legal standards, and the universal ethical principles often fail people who must make right-versus-right choices that will shape others' lives and their own as well.

The tale of an Eastern sage and his young disciple illustrates the problem. The young man asked, "O Wise Man, what holds up the earth?" The sage responded, "The answer, my son, is a very strong man." After some thought, the young man asked, "What holds up the strong man?" The sage responded, "A large stone, my son." After further reflection, the young man returned and asked what held up the stone. The sage, growing impatient, said, "A turtle, my son." When the young man persisted and asked, "What supports the turtle?" the Wise Man snapped, "Look, kid, from there on it's turtles all the way down."

WARM AND BREATHING TRUTHS

Grand principles have another serious shortcoming: they are cold and impersonal. People seeking what the American philosopher Charles Peirce called "a warm and breathing truth," a belief that will animate and shape their lives, are naturally disappointed by these carefully crafted, but austere abstractions. Right-versus-right decisions are often choices about life, not opportunities for technical analysis.

Put yourself in the following situation. You are standing in front of a burning building. You realize that you can run to one part of the building and save a single child, or you can run to another part and save three children. In neither case is there any risk to you. But there is no way to save everyone. You must choose between saving three children and saving one.

At this point, certain grand principles are marginally useful. If you actually need reasons to act—rather than do nothing and watch all the children die—the principles will provide them. The greatest good for the greatest number is saving three children rather than one. So the right thing is clear. You begin running toward the three children. But you glance once more at the child standing alone and realize that she is your daughter. What choice do you make now?

The grand principles have now become confusing. Three lives still count more than one. Like your child, the three have a right to life, and you have a duty to save them.* But you also have a basic duty as a parent to protect your child from danger. In addition

---

* This is a highly simplified account of the philosophical analysis of this situation. In fact, this type of problem has been debated for centuries and interpreted in a multitude of ways, depending on which interpretation from which school of ethical theory is brought to bear.

to the confusion, something now seems deeply wrong. The grand principles seem to be asking you to subordinate your decision—indeed, some of your deepest loyalties—to an abstract analysis of impersonal duties. You are asked, it seems, to ignore the sort of profound emotional commitment—in this case, a parent's to a child—that gives life meaning.[15]

Given this drawback of the grand principles, on top of all the others, it is no surprise that people look elsewhere for ethical guidance. Writing in the eighteenth century, the Scottish philosopher David Hume suggested that the sane reaction to a philosophical morass was to climb out, clean oneself off, go home, have a good dinner, and forget all about philosophy.[16] As rationality endlessly chases its tail, people decide that principled reasoning can't help them very much.

Many people believe they have found a simple, user-friendly alternative to moral philosophy, corporate law, and company mission statements. They find no prospect of simplicity on the other side of all these complexities. So, instead of relying on objective external principles, they look for answers within themselves, in their moral intuitions and instincts, and practice what can be called "sleep-test ethics."

To the classic view that the unexamined life is not worth living, sleep-test ethics replies that the overexamined life isn't much good either. Self-expression, spontaneity, authenticity, and being true to one's self—all these make sleep-test ethics a compelling alternative to long, cerebral, often-frustrating searches for the right grand principles. Its basic idea is that, if people can sleep well after making a difficult ethical decision, they have probably made the right choice. Is this so?

4

↔

Sleep-Test Ethics

W HEN PEOPLE DISCUSS MORAL DILEMMAS, they often refer to "sleep tests" and "wake-up calls." These have somehow become important metaphors for thinking about difficult ethical problems. For example, one young woman, working as a loan officer at a major bank, faced relentless pressure from her boss to approve a dubious loan for a pal of his. She described her reaction by saying, "It was a real wake-up call. I thought, Oh my God, this isn't theory. This is life." Wake-up calls, it seems, can shake people out of a naive slumber and signal that something fundamental is at stake in a situation.

The sleep test appears to work differently. It is supposed to tell people whether or not they have made a morally sound decision. In its literal version, a person who has made the right choice can sleep soundly afterward; someone who has made the wrong choice cannot. Lady Macbeth, for example, awoke in the dead of night, tormented by guilt because she and her husband had murdered several of his political rivals. In doing so, Shakespeare says, they also "murder'd sleep."

Defined less literally and more broadly, sleep-test ethics rests on a single, fundamental belief: that we should rely on our personal insights, feelings, and instincts when we face a difficult ethical problem. Defined this way, sleep-test ethics is the ethics of intuition. It advises us to follow our hearts, particularly when our minds are confused. It says that, if something continues to gnaw at us, it probably should. More than 100 years ago, Ralph Waldo Emerson, the American writer and popular philosopher, wrote his famous essay "Self-Reliance" and told his readers, "Trust thyself: every heart vibrates to that iron string."[1]

For many people, "trust thyself" is a compelling way of resolving difficult ethical issues. They believe strongly in following their ethical instincts, because these instincts have been nurtured and shaped by their families, their religious beliefs, or other experiences, relationships, and commitments that are vital parts of their lives. Hence, we must ask whether sleep-test ethics can help managers who must resolve right-versus-right problems.

The answer to this question is complicated and very important, because we must tease apart two competing versions of sleep-test ethics. One is the foundation for a powerful, practical way of thinking about right-versus-right problems. The other, especially for managers, is a path to disaster. Unfortunately, the two versions of sleep-test ethics look quite alike. Both rely heavily on instincts. Both use physical and emotional distress as indicators that something is morally amiss. Both seem to say, "Trust yourself." How, then, do we distinguish the valid version of sleep-test ethics from its counterfeit?

ME-ISM

To answer these questions, we will turn to the Greek philosopher Aristotle. He spent years thinking about the role that intuition, emotion, and personal judgment should play in resolving practical ethical problems. Imagine, for a moment, that Aristotle could spend six months in the United States. Suppose that he watched television, visited schools, shopped at the mall, and attended various religious services—all with the aim of understanding how Americans live and how they think about ethical issues. What might he conclude?

This question may seem to invite little more than speculation. After all, Aristotle lived long ago, between 384 and 322 B.C. Little is known about his early life: some accounts describe a period of "riotous living"; others, a more somber and inspiring boyhood.[2] Moreover, the classical culture Aristotle knew—that of Athens, a small Greek city-state—differed greatly from the culture of modern or postmodern America. But much of what Aristotle wrote has survived, both physically and intellectually. We have, for example, his lecture notes on ethics, called *The Nichomachean Ethics*. And we have his ideas, not as exhibits in museums of antiquity, but as sources of continuing insight for philosophers, psychologists, theologians, and others, who reflect on his ideas and use them to understand contemporary ethical issues.

Aristotle studied and lived in Plato's Academy for many years. There he learned and taught Plato's philosophy and then modified it profoundly. Plato believed that true reality consists of unchanging, flawless entities—such as perfect justice, perfect truth, and perfect beauty—which he called "the eternal forms." (The search for universal grand principles is a Platonic endeavor.) The eternal forms can be known only through our intellects. In contrast, in our everyday lives, we muck about with imperfect versions of the eternal forms, because we rely so heavily on the crude instruments of our senses.

Aristotle took a different approach: he refused to dismiss the reports of our senses as mere shadows of reality. He had a scientist's instinctive regard for empirical detail. He loved to watch, examine, investigate, and classify. Hence, the prospect of studying contemporary Americans—a people unlike any he had ever encountered—would surely have excited him.

What if Aristotle, while studying the United States, did something a colleague and I did recently, and asked a group of thoughtful men and women, mostly in their late twenties, to describe how they would resolve difficult ethical dilemmas?[3] Many of the answers we heard were versions of sleep-test ethics. Here are some typical comments:

Just do what's right. Do what you believe is right.

This sounds hokey, but it's how you feel. If something makes you feel bad, that's untenable.

You need to draw upon your own experiences and values. You use these as a compass. These should be the guiding light.

I guess my thought is, How does it make you feel? If you're getting sick all the time, that tells you something. The bottom line is what you're comfortable with.

Behind these four comments is a view of the world that the Canadian author Douglas Coupland called, in his novel *Generation X,* "me-ism." This is a "search by an individual, in the absence of training in traditional religious tenets, to formulate a personally tailored religion by himself."[4] Note that "me-ism" does not mean selfishness; it refers to a customized, composite personal faith.

Me-ism even seems to be spreading across the globe. For example, Kenichi Ohmai, a prominent Japanese business consultant and writer, has described contemporary Japanese teenagers as a Nintendo generation. They are responding to a powerful subliminal message of videogames: "one can take active control of one's situation and change one's fate. No one need submit passively to authority. Everything can be explored, rearranged, and reprogrammed. Nothing has to be fixed or final."[5]

Aristotle would probably find all this very troubling. For one thing, the four students' comments and the me-ism they represent seem to sanctify individuals' intuitions. Although Aristotle believed that intuition was a valuable guide to ethical problems, he did not think that a moral intuition, however clear and heartfelt, could certify its own moral soundness.

Everyone knows people who sleep quite soundly even though they have the ethics of bottom-dwelling slugs. They may be masters of rationalization or denial, they may be sociopaths and lack a conscience, but they can look themselves in the mirror and live in peace with whatever perfidy they have committed. During the Holocaust, a good number of doctors spent their days committing atrocities in the concentration camps, and then sat down to quiet family dinners.

In contrast, responsible people sometimes lie awake at night *precisely because they have done the right thing.* They understand that their decisions have real consequences, that success is not guaranteed, and that they will be held accountable for their decisions. They also understand that acting honorably and decently can, in some circumstances, complicate or damage a person's career. In short, if people like Hitler sometimes sleep well and if people like Mother Teresa sometimes sleep badly, we can place little faith in simple sleep-test ethics.

Aristotle would also be disturbed by the individualism—indeed, the hyperindividualism—underlying me-ism. It reflects the crudely egalitarian worldview, "You're entitled to your views and I'm entitled to mine." He would no doubt be stunned by comments like the one a student of mine made to his wife: "Look, just do what you think is right. You're 25. You don't have to answer to anyone."

Notice the social and ethical restraints on individual behavior that the four representative comments and me-ism *do not include.* Aristotle believed that four great virtues—courage, justice, prudence, and temperance—should govern human behavior. All are missing and unaccounted for here. So, too, are the ethics of duties or the ethics of consequences, the Ten Commandments, the Golden Rule, and other tenets of organized religion.[6]

One other consideration would also trouble Aristotle: the society and culture that have shaped me-ism. Aristotle trusted individual judgment, as long as the individual had a sound moral character. But sound character, in his mind, derived from growing up in a community that respected his four virtues and trained young people to think and act in accordance with them. Hence, Aristotle might not place much confidence in the instinctive judgments of a 25-year-old like Steve Lewis or a 35-year-old like Peter Adario—after having observed the pervasive role of television in contemporary life. The average American child, for example, sees 18,000 murders on television by the age of 16, and 350,000 commercials by the age of 18.[7] In a society in which many people can recite more commercial jingles than prayers and poems, Aristotle might be reluctant to give too much weight to spontaneous moral sentiments. One young man explained the problem to me in these terms: he feared that, when he faced a difficult problem and looked deep into his soul, he would find mostly reruns of "Gilligan's Island" and 'The Brady Bunch."

THE BOTTOM LINE

Suppose that a manager asked Aristotle, as he neared the end of his sojourn in America, for his "bottom line" on the version of sleep-test ethics we have been discussing. He would likely respond with three comments.

The first is that it makes little sense to tell business managers to follow their ethical instincts in right-versus-right situations. A basic feature of these problems is that the men and women who must solve them are pulled in different directions by their ethical instincts. This was the problem for Rebecca Dennet, Steve Lewis, Peter Adario, and Edouard Sakiz. In these cases, intuition did not point to the answer, but highlighted the difficulty of the problem.

Second, even if managers' intuitions seem to give a strong, clear indication of the right thing to do, they should not leap into action. Even if some pure ethical signal is transmitted from deep in the human heart, it can easily be distorted—by an individual's wants and needs, by the surrounding culture, and by the pressures and demands of an organization. A thoughtful manager cannot simply ask: What is my moral intuition about the problem in front of me? Other questions also need answering: How can I really know what my moral instinct is in a complicated, uncertain situation? How do I know that I'm not rationalizing or denying important elements of the situation? Will my intuition lead me across the boundaries defined by the law and by basic moral principles?

The final problem with the sleep test is that managers, like others in positions of power in a society, must explain and justify their decisions in terms that others can understand. They are not high priests reading entrails. Even if a manager has a firm, clear, authentic ethical instinct about a particular problem, he or she can't simply announce, "This is my decision. My heart tells me it's right, and I know I can live with it, so there it is." Managers are accountable for explaining their decisions and for describing why their responsibilities have led them in a particular direction. And, if they expect others to follow them, their explanation must be convincing and compelling.

In short, the counterfeit version of sleep-test ethics is a close cousin of Ernest Hemingway's view that "I only know that moral is

what you feel good after and immoral is what you feel bad after."[8]
It relies on simple, quick, highly subjective, intensely individualistic,
and allegedly self-validating personal reactions to ethical problems.
Aristotle would vigorously reject this approach to ethical problems.
He would warn managers, and everyone else, that it is a snare and
a delusion.

EXPLOITING THE INEVITABLE

At this point in the analysis, sleep-test ethics seems to be buried
under an avalanche of powerful criticisms. Why bother to dig it
out? There are two reasons for doing so. The first, which is examined
in this section, is that we must be realistic about sleep-test ethics.
We cannot outlaw it, because human beings will almost inevitably
rely on their intuition when they face difficult moral decisions.

We do so because we are beings of a particular kind: creatures
of flesh and blood, spirit and emotion—not calculating machines.
As the old adage puts it, "We see the world not as it is, but as we
are." The grand principles try to wring the feelings, gut instincts,
and intuitions out of ethical decisions. A better alternative is to
understand the near-inevitability of such feelings and find ways to
turn them to our advantage. Aristotle understood this, as have almost
all religious leaders.

The other reason to reconsider sleep-test ethics, which is examined in the next section, is that intuition can play a valuable role
when managers must resolve right-versus-right issues. As we have
seen, these problems have significant personal and emotional dimensions. Sleep-test ethics recognizes these vital aspects of serious ethical issues and draws insight and guidance from them.

The crucial issue is not *whether* we should rely on our ethical
intuitions, but *how* to do so—thoughtfully and responsibly. Sleep-
test ethics is both inevitable and potentially valuable, given the kind
of creatures we are and the kind of problems we sometimes face.

What accounts for the near-inevitability of sleep-test ethics? A
good way to begin answering this question is by examining an
extraordinary example of sleep-test ethics and business ethics. This
is the heroism of Oskar Schindler, the German businessman made

famous by Steven Spielberg's highly acclaimed film *Schindler's List.*
During the Nazi occupation of Poland and Czechoslovakia, Schindler owned and managed two factories. He persuaded the Nazis to
designate them as labor camps, and then he ran the factories as safe
havens for more than a thousand Jews. Schindler's efforts saved them
from almost-certain death, in Auschwitz or another concentration
camp, and put his own life at grave risk.

How did Schindler—lapsed Catholic, *bon vivant,* chronic adulterer,
and war profiteer—rise to these moral heights? What led him to
risk his life, not just once in a single heroic act, but day after day,
month after month, for more than three years? The answer seems
to be that Schindler simply knew what was right, and he knew it
directly, swiftly, and intuitively. This conclusion emerges from a
process of elimination. Nothing in Schindler's life presaged his brave
deeds. Moreover, Thomas Keneally, who wrote the book on
which Spielberg's film is based, interviewed many of the people
Schindler rescued; none of them had heard Schindler explain his
actions.[9]

Steven Spielberg was also puzzled about Schindler's motives. His
response was to create, out of whole cloth, a decisive scene for his
film. It shows Oskar Schindler, on top of a hill, watching the brutal
liquidation of the Cracow ghetto by Nazi troopers. For several
seconds, his eyes follow a little girl as she wanders alone through
the mayhem and savagery. Spielberg suggests that some such incident was a wake-up call for Oskar Schindler, which led him to stop
exploiting the Jews who worked in his businesses and begin rescuing
them instead.

This story suggests why sleep-test ethics is such a compelling
way of resolving difficult ethical problems. First, sleep-test ethics is
deeply personal. It relies on "warm, breathing truths," rather than
on abstract, incorporeal principles. It banks on truths and commitments that are validated, not by principles presented in a book, but
their resonance with a person's whole self. This approach follows
Nietzsche's plea, "Oh, my friends, that your self be in your deed as
the mother is in her child—let that be *your* word concerning virtue."[10]
This seems to describe Schindler, who was literally prepared to live
and die for his choices.

Sleep-test ethics seems to accept that difficult ethical choices are often important life choices. It encourages people to ground decisions in their core intuitions, passions, and commitments, rather than in principles and calculations. A mother who sees her child inside a burning building is justified in running in and saving her, rather than three other children, if that is what her heart tells her she must do.

The second attraction of the sleep test is its optimism. It helps people feel better about themselves and about human nature, because it supposes that morally good actions are natural and comfortable, that we can trust our instincts, and that we will somehow know or sense what is right and wrong.

The third reason that the ethics of intuition is so compelling is that it may be hard-wired; that is, the confidence in human nature that underlies sleep-test ethics may well have biological origins. What humans, chimpanzees, moles, bees, termites, sponges, slime molds, and innumerable other creatures have in common is that they all create complex societies. This suggests something akin to a moral instinct.[11]

In fact, scientists may soon be able to pinpoint the location of moral instincts in the human brain. A crude indicator of their position resulted from the cruel accident suffered by a railroad worker named Phineas Gage in 1848. An explosion drove an iron rod into his left cheek, through the base of his skull, and out the top of his head. Miraculously, Gage survived. His mental skills remained intact, but unfortunately his character did not. Before the accident, he was a reputable, hard-working family man; afterward, he became an undisciplined, foul-mouthed drifter. The rod had apparently destroyed the parts of the brain that govern morality.[12]

Definitive proof of scientific theories about moral instincts lies in the future. But, until then, the past will continue to legitimate sleep-test ethics. In other words, the fourth reason for the power and appeal of sleep-test ethics is cultural. As we will see, Aristotle was the intellectual forefather of sleep-test ethics—at least of the meaningful version of it. In the Western tradition, this is a powerful cultural mandate. Moreover, Americans seem to have a special affinity for this approach to ethics. Sociologist Robert Bellah's widely acclaimed book *Habits of the Heart* shows that, for generations, Americans have been evolving a worldview that he calls "expressive individualism." This is the idea that "each person has a unique core of feeling and intuition that should unfold or be expressed if individuality is to be realized."[13]

This way of thinking is hardly unique to the United States. It originated in Europe with the Romantic movement of the eighteenth century. It migrated to America, where each generation has rediscovered these ideas and made them its own. In the middle of the last century, Emerson said, "Trust thyself." Shortly after the middle of this century, people "let it all hang out" and "did their own thing." Now, at the end of the century, Nike ads exhort, "Just do it." And, like this slogan, expressive individualism is now spreading around the globe, propelled by the seemingly indomitable force of American popular culture.

The final attraction of the sleep test is that it seems extraordinarily practical. Oskar Schindler didn't get tangled up in debates about grand principles. His moral instincts seemed to provide a shortcut that was uncomplicated and user friendly, simple and direct. In short, thoughtful people do not turn casually to sleep-test ethics. They are responding to powerful, deep-rooted forces that are cultural, psychological, emotional, practical, and perhaps even biological. Each of these is strong, and each reinforces the others.

Hence, it is simply unrealistic to expect people—especially when they face difficult, distressing decisions—to rise above their culture, their history, their hopes and fears, their personal commitments, their religious faiths, their urgent need for practical assistance, their biological predispositions—in a word, their humanity—and enter an abstract, Platonic realm of dispassionate ethical analysis.

Aristotle understood our deeply ingrained tendency to refract ethical issues through the prism of personal feelings, concerns, experiences, and instincts. His moral philosophy was not written for androids, the science fiction creatures that look like human beings but are actually computers. Aristotle's moral philosophy deals extensively with the development of moral character and with ways of refining the intuitions that so often and so powerfully envelop our moral reflection.[14] This is, in essence, a strategy of exploiting the inevitable.

ARISTOTLE'S SLEEP TEST

The ethics of intuition is not only inevitable, or nearly so. It is also the right approach to resolving right-versus-right issues. Interpreted this way, sleep-test ethics is a test of integrity. To understand this, it is important to reflect on a fundamental characteristic of right-versus-right problems.

Recall Steve Lewis's problem and notice the ways in which it was *his* problem and no one else's. The colleagues who asked him to go to St. Louis, simply because he was black, didn't think there was a problem. Andy Webster, Lewis's mentor, realized that there might be a problem for Lewis but didn't hesitate to offer to take Lewis's place in St. Louis. (If situations like this had ever been a problem for Webster, he had by now apparently come to terms with them.) So why was there a problem for Lewis? After all, everyone involved in the situation seemed to be facing the same set of facts. Why was Lewis the only one with a problem?

The answer is that he had a problem because of who he was, because of his values, commitments, experiences, hopes, and fears. His list of pros and cons makes this very clear. Most white investment bankers would not have written "Malcolm" on their list of cons. Some might not have even understood that Lewis was referring to Malcolm X. None would have known that Lewis was referring, in particular, to the difference between house slaves and field slaves, or to the harsh comment passed along to Lewis about his decision to become an investment banker, or that when Lewis wrote "Malcolm" he feared selling out or, more precisely, being an "oreo."

Had Lewis finished his list, the next step would have been to assign weights to each consideration. This, too, is a personal matter. Each member of Lewis's firm might have had a different set of priorities—depending, once again, on who they were. There is no single, objective table of moral weights and measures for everyone to use. At the core of a right-versus-right dilemma are personal values, choices, commitments, and risks. Once again, the adage "We see the world not as it is, but as we are" is apt.

Aristotle's approach to ethics leaves ample room for intuitions, feelings, and other personal considerations. Instead of following the grand principles, which tell people "Know the rules," he follows the ancient advice, which says, "Know thyself." Aristotle did not merely accept or tolerate the role of intuition in ethical decisions. Nor did he simply exploit their inevitability. He prized them because he believed they could penetrate to the essence of an issue.

One of his most distinguished modern interpreters, Martha Nussbaum, has written that, for Aristotle, the emotions—a large element of our intuition—are frequently "more reliable in deliberation than detached intellectual judgments."[15] Another eminent Aristotelian, Stuart Hampshire, writes that, in Aristotle's mind, ethical behavior "should not be the outcome of careful and laborious calculation and reflection; it should be immediate, spontaneous, governed by intuition."[16]

In short, Aristotle endorsed a version of sleep-test ethics—as long as it met his criteria. And what were they? They are precisely the criteria that would have led him to denounce me-ism. The development of character is crucial: a sound ethical instinct presupposes a thoughtful, mature person. The ethical instinct is not just a single, compelling impulse. Nor is it a substitute for common sense, logic, or consideration of basic ethical principles. The intuition arises after serious attention to the relevant facts, not in place of them. The intuition does not lead a person across the boundary between right and wrong defined by the grand principles. Finally, a sound ethical intuition can be articulated and explained to others in ways that draw on important social and ethical practices in a society.

For people who want precise guidelines, Aristotle's criteria are dismayingly vague. What is a "mature" person? What is an "important social practice"? How much attention is "serious" attention to the facts? Aristotle doesn't say. He did not believe it was possible to be precise and specific about matters like these; far too much depends on the situation and the person.

The looseness of these criteria frustrates some people but liberates others.[17] It gives them freedom—to reflect on who they are and what they hope to become, to feel and act on what they care most deeply about, to make commitments and try to live by them. This freedom is not, of course, a framework for resolving right-versus-right conflicts. But it is a crucial first step in this direction.

A FRAMEWORK FOR REFLECTION

The framework of phrases and questions presented in the remaining chapters of this book offers subsequent steps for resolving right-versus-right conflicts. It provides a way to avoid the pitfalls of the quickie version of sleep-test ethics—without sacrificing the engagement, richness, and power of this age-old way of thinking about important choices in life. The framework here does not offer the ultimate, all-purpose analytical tool or an updated model of the ethics machine. Instead, it illuminates critical dimensions of right-versus-right problems through the use of important phrases and passages from the writing of realistic, practical-minded moralists—chief among them, our friend Aristotle; Niccolo Machiavelli, the Renaissance political philosopher; Nietzsche; and William James.

This approach builds on Aristotle's empiricism, rather than Plato's abstractions, for resolving difficult ethical decisions. It shifts the focus of ethical deliberation from abstract principles to issues of personal character, from logic toward psychology, from the universal to the individual, from the intellectual toward the emotional, from objective truths to personal choice and commitment, and from the marble temple on the hill to the hurly-burly of everyday life. In all these ways, the perspective of this framework is much closer to literature than to the grand principles.[18]

The framework of phrases is not a substitute for the grand principles; they remain important, sometimes crucial, because they define the boundaries between right and wrong. But when conflicts occur within these boundaries, managers need a way of thinking that can help them resolve these problems in ways they can live with.

Our search now is for practical guidance on these problems. We are proceeding in the spirit William James endorses in his book *Pragmatism.* There he writes, "Most of us have a hankering for the good things on both sides of the line. Facts are good, of course—give us lots of facts. Principles are good—give us plenty of principles."[19]

5

↔

Defining Moments

A RECENT NOVEL, *The Remains of the Day*, describes the reflections of a British butler, Stevens, who is traveling through the British countryside and struggling to come to peace with his career and his life.[1] The life of a 60-year-old butler may seem an odd source of lessons about contemporary life and the difficult decisions managers must sometimes make. Yet the author, Kazuo Ishiguro, thought otherwise and once explained his choice of a main character by saying simply, "We are all butlers."[2]

During his travels, Stevens spends much of his time thinking back on a handful of choices, some made 25 years earlier, that irrevocably shaped his life and career. As he recalls these decisions, Stevens sometimes feels pride, more often sorrow. Most painful, perhaps, is his realization that he didn't understand all that was at stake when he made his life-shaping choices. Only now, looking back, does he see how, during a few precious moments, he held his life in his hands and irrevocably defined its course.

Stevens's choices were defining moments. So, too, are the right-versus-right decisions that managers must sometimes make. Rebecca Dennet, Steve Lewis, Peter Adario, and Edouard Sakiz all stood at a crossroads. Important values, personal and professional, pointed in different directions. Neither the grand principles nor their ethical intuitions could give them the right answer. The pressure was intense; much was uncertain. Like Stevens, they could easily misjudge what was really at stake, for themselves and others, and make choices they would long regret. Such risks are unavoidable, for managers and for anyone else with serious responsibilities for others' lives.

Fortunately, however, there are ways to load the dice in favor of practical, responsible decisions—choices that managers can look back on with a sense of achievement, pride, and honor. The first step in this direction is understanding the ways in which right-versus-right decisions are defining moments in managers' lives and careers.

THE APEX OF A CAREER

John Dewey, the American philosopher and educator, provides us with a powerful and insightful starting point. In his book *Ethics*, written in 1908, Dewey writes that important ethical decisions have two important aspects. The public side is what other people can observe, such as a person's actions and their consequences. The private side, in contrast, is more subtle. In Dewey's phrase, it involves the ways in which ethical decisions "form, reveal, and test the self."[3] Dewey's phrase is brief—only six short words—yet it casts a powerful, illuminating light on what is at stake when managers make right-versus-right choices and the basic ways in which these choices are defining moments. We will see shortly how *revealing*, *testing*, and *shaping* are key elements of defining moments.

Although *The Remains of the Day* is set in 1956, when Stevens is nearing retirement, its crucial events occur in the years between the two world wars, when Stevens served as a butler to a British lord named Darlington. The defining moment in Stevens's career occurred on the last evening of an important international conference at Darlington Hall. Lord Darlington and others were orchestrating an extremely delicate set of negotiations, aimed at persuading the French government to lighten the sanctions imposed on Germany after World War I.

Stevens viewed the conference as the apex of his career. He had spent years striving to become a great butler, an aspiration that he defined in unambiguously ethical terms. A great butler, in his mind, embodied the quality of dignity. And dignity represented an ethic of self-sacrifice and noble service. A great butler devoted his entire self to filling his professional role and performing his duties. The butler did so in the service of a morally good master, which Stevens believed Darlington to be. And the master, in turn, had to be devoted to some larger cause—in this case, humane treatment for the vanquished and impoverished Germans. At one point, Stevens says, "My vocation will not be fulfilled until I have done all I can to see his lordship through the great tasks he has set for himself."

By the final evening of the conference, there had been some progress. The French representative seemed open minded about the proposals under discussion. Stevens knew this and felt deeply proud of his contribution to these developments. For years, he had trained the large staff of Darlington Hall for such an event. For weeks before the conference, he had worked ceaselessly, as a "general might prepare for battle." He told the staff that "history could be made under this roof." During the conference, Stevens even found time to provide comfort and medical attention for the French delegate, whose feet were badly blistered. All in all, he stood at the threshold of a resounding achievement, professionally and personally.

But Stevens's father, who was also employed at Darlington Hall, lay dying in a room upstairs. Earlier that day, he had suffered a devastating stroke. Thus Stevens had to choose between sitting at his father's bedside and overseeing the crucial final hours of the conference. Stevens visited his father briefly and then returned to his professional duties.

Just after dinner, while Stevens was serving drinks to the guests, Miss Kenton, the housekeeper at Darlington Hall, took him aside. She told him that his father had just passed away. Miss Kenton asks if Stevens will come upstairs. He responds that he will do so in a few moments, adding, "You see, I know my father would have wished me to carry on just now." Later in the story, Stevens tells us, "For all its sad associations, whenever I recall that evening today, I find I do so with a large sense of triumph." He believed he had finally measured up to the exacting standards of service that he had set for himself. Now, he believed, he could compare himself to the great butlers of his era, including his own father.

There is more to this story, and we will return to it soon. At this point, however, it is important to examine what Stevens's decision tells us about the revealing, testing, and shaping that are the core elements of a defining moment. In reality, a single choice or action, like Steven's decision, fuses all three elements. They do not unfold, one by one, as tidy, separate stages or discrete choices. Nevertheless, it is valuable to look closely at each element of a defining moment.

REVEALING

In a variety of ways, some quite powerful, defining moments reveal. They may surface something hidden. They can crystallize what was fluid and unformed. They may give a sharp, clear view of something previously obscure. In every case, however, a defining moment reveals something important about a person's basic values and about his or her abiding commitments in life.

Chester Barnard held this view. His years of business experience led him to conclude that the moral codes of a typical manager were "ingrained in him by causes, forces, experiences, which he has either forgotten or on the whole never recognized. Just what they are, in fact, can at best only be approximately inferred from his actions, preferably under stress."[4] Defining moments compel people to arrange their values in single file and reveal the priorities among them.

Stevens chose to remain at the conference, rather than sit by his father's bedside. In doing so, he showed that he cared, first and foremost, about his professional ideals. When he chose to carry on with his duties after dinner, rather than go upstairs and close his father's eyes, he told Miss Kenton that he was doing what he believed his father would have wished him to do. In saying this, he revealed something more: his rationale for his values. Stevens had a personal, carefully crafted interpretation of the lives his father and other great butlers had lived, and he had worked fervently to join their ranks.

Not all defining moments take precisely the same form as Stevens's. A choice may reveal little to others but a great deal to the person who makes it. These moments of clarity are private and personal. In other cases, a choice can reveal more to others, if they are thoughtful and observant, than to the person who makes it. Still other choices, like Stevens's, reveal a good deal to others. His decision, like the rest of his life, was exceedingly deliberate, and he gave Miss Kenton the reason for his decision. And, in all likelihood, staff of the house quickly learned what Stevens had done. His values were there for the world to see.

Defining moments need not take place in a moment or a brief episode. Stevens did have to react immediately, once he learned his father had died. The young investment banker, Steve Lewis, had only an hour or so to decide what to do about the St. Louis meeting. In contrast, however, Peter Adario had several days to decide how to resolve the conflict between Kathryn McNeil and Lisa Walters, and Edouard Sakiz had much longer to decide how to proceed with RU 486.

Although Stevens's decision isn't the template for all defining moments, it does underscore several important aspects of these decisions and what they reveal. There is, for example, no guarantee that a defining moment will unveil a value or commitment that is morally inspiring or elevating. Hitler, no doubt, had defining moments, as do everyday scoundrels and humbugs. Many people react to Stevens's defining moment by shaking their heads in sorrow.

Moreover, what is revealed in a defining moment is rarely a startling new facet of an individual's personality. Long before his choice on the final evening of the conference, Stevens had revealed his abiding values and commitments—through innumerable acts of scrupulous, self-effacing attention to the minute details of household management. These brief moments of self-disclosure confirmed the observation of Michel de Montaigne, the great French essayist of the sixteenth century, that a single gesture, if one observed it closely enough, could reveal a person's entire character. Defining moments reveal by crystallizing. They are sharper, more vivid, more intensified versions of what a person has been revealing, usually in small ways, almost every day.

Another basic feature of a defining moment is that it reveals as much about a person's past as it does about a present choice. People can reveal who they are and what they care about only if they are already someone. Stevens did not come to his defining moment as what one philosopher has called an "unencumbered self."[5] He was not a blank slate on which he could sketch whatever portrait of himself he pleased. Each of us is, like Stevens, largely what we have been. In this respect, the warning on passenger-side rear-view mirrors—"Objects in mirror are closer than they appear"—reads as a statement about life and its defining moments.

Finally, Stevens's decision is also a reminder that defining moments, though deeply personal, are also profoundly social. They open windows, not only on individuals' lives and experiences, but also on the values of the communities in which they have lived. Aristotle's most famous statement is his definition of a human being. In his *Politics*, he wrote that "Man is by nature a political animal"—a creature, that is, of the *polis* or surrounding society. Later in *Politics*, Aristotle is even more emphatic, writing that "He who is unable to live in society, or who has no need because he is sufficient for himself, must be either a beast or a god."[6]

Stevens's life, literally and figuratively, was confined within the walls of Darlington Hall, a microcosm of the politics, manners, and social relations of British society between the world wars. Hence, Stevens's choice revealed not only his character, but that of the society around him. Defining moments reveal the political as well as the personal.

TESTING

Stevens's decisions on the evening of his father's death were also a *test* of his values. This is the second crucial aspect of defining moments. It is also the most familiar. All moral choices, even the most obvious cases of right versus wrong, test a person's values. They indicate whether someone is really committed to particular values or only gives them lip service.

However, right-versus-right choices are particularly demanding tests, because people must choose between two or more values to which they are deeply and genuinely committed. In other words, the price of loyalty to some values and commitments is the sacrifice of others. Stevens, for example, believed that he faced a right-versus-right choice. For him, the basic question was whether he could summon the strength to serve his master and the grand cause to which his master was dedicated—at the very moment when his father, to whom he felt deep obligations, had just passed away. Although Stevens was a master at repressing his feelings, tears ran down his cheeks when he returned to the smoking room after learning of his father's death. He was paying a very high price for pursuing his high ideals of professional service.

Stevens faced a professional and personal challenge that many managers can recognize. (This may be one sense in which Ishiguro believes "We are all butlers.") The pressure was on. Stevens had important professional responsibilities. His goals were clear, and he was measuring himself against exacting standards. He didn't have the time to think everything through. Above all, Stevens's personal and family responsibilities clashed painfully with his professional aspirations and what he believed to be his professional obligations.

All of the business managers we have been discussing faced defining tests. Peter Adario, for example, believed he had an obligation to help Kathryn McNeil keep her job and at the same time take care of her son. As events unfolded, however, he would learn that he would have to run serious professional risks to translate his praiseworthy goal into reality. In this way, his values and commitments would be seriously tested.

SHAPING

For Stevens, the final evening of the conference was more than a test. What mattered to him above all was that he had become (or so he fervently hoped) a particular kind of person. He cared deeply that his actions—and, much more importantly for him, his character—truly embodied the highest ideals of self-sacrifice and professional service.* Decades later, when he recalled the conference, he did so with deep pride because he believed it was the moment when he *became* a great butler.

The third basic aspect of a defining moment is that it can shape a person. Some of this shaping involves uneventful, minor decisions or actions. Looking at these one at a time is deceptive. Cumulatively, however, they form character, just as drops of water eventually reshape a stone. Late-night infomercials on cable television may offer quick self-transformation, but life ordinarily does not. Aristotle's view is more plausible. "A state of character," he wrote, "arises from the repetition of similar activities."[7]

No one was shocked when Stevens remained at the conference instead of going to his father's bedside. His choice did not make him a new person, but it did shape him, insofar as he reaffirmed and further entrenched some of his basic traits. His decision helped him become "more himself." In this respect, his choice, like every choice people make, shaped his character in a particular way.

Other choices are more dramatic and shape one more powerfully. Stevens's choice crystallized a compelling image of himself, and this became the lens through which he interpreted his life. Stevens believed that, through his choice, he had become a great or near-great butler. His life had begun in obscurity; he worked very hard for many years; and now, finally, he had become someone. Henceforth he would see the world, and expect the world to see him, not as a mere servant, but as a man of dignity and stature. This self-image remained firmly in place for two decades. He did not reconsider it until he suffered several grievous personal disappointments. Only then did his view of himself as a great butler weaken its hold on his life.

---

* Another important aspect of Stevens's character—his moral blindness—stood at odds with his high ideals of service. At one point, for example, Lord Darlington asked him to dismiss two Jewish maids, because their employment could disturb high-ranking officials of the German government who sometimes visited Darlington Hall. Stevens did so, without qualms or hesitation, because he believed it his duty to carry out his master's wishes. His devotion also blinded him to indications that his master had become an unwitting pawn of German foreign policy.

There is a third way in which a defining moment can shape a person's life. It can be a turning point, a forking of the road. Dewey mentions, as examples, "the choice of a calling in life or of a life-partner."[8] These decisions and others are choices of a way of life. Stevens chose the life of a devoted butler—in the service, he believed, of noble ends—rather than a life as a husband and perhaps a parent. Most people understand the seriousness of these decisions at the time they make them. In some cases, such as marriage, society underscores the importance of a decision through formal ceremonies and commitments.

But there are other defining moments, with equally important consequences, that seem minor when they happen. Most people can recall choices like these. They open certain doors and close others, sometimes forever. They change a person by changing the person's life and experiences.

One of Stevens's painful disappointments began with what seemed to be a small decision. During the years after the international conference, he and Miss Kenton, the chief housekeeper, worked together closely. She came to have strong feelings for him, although he was only faintly aware of them. A great butler, as Stevens now believed himself to be, simply did not indulge such feelings. Moreover, he was busy with the grand task of serving Lord Darlington, who continued his efforts to repair British-German relations.

One day, Stevens found himself standing outside Miss Kenton's room and heard her weeping. She had just learned that her aunt had died. He could have knocked on her door and gone in to comfort her. Instead, he walked away because he was reluctant, as he put it, to "intrude upon her private grief." Soon, he forgot the incident.

But, later in his life, this seemingly inconsequential decision began to trouble him. Not long after the incident, Miss Kenton left Darlington Hall to marry a man she did not love. Here are Stevens's painful reflections on these events, 20 years later:

> But what is the sense in forever speculating what might have happened had such and such a moment turned out differently? One could presumably drive oneself to distraction in this way. In any case, while it is all very

well to talk of "turning points," one can surely only recognize such moments in retrospect. Naturally, when one looks back to such instances today, they may indeed take on the appearance of being crucial, precious moments in one's life; but of course, at the time, this was not the impression one had. . . . There was surely nothing to indicate at the time that such evidently small incidents would render whole dreams forever irredeemable.[9]

What Stevens lost was his dream of a life with Miss Kenton. The end of the novel describes his brief visit with her and the end of his hope that she will return to Darlington Hall. She chooses to return to her estranged husband, and Stevens is left alone, contemplating the remains of his days.

DEFINING MOMENTS, MANAGERS, AND ORGANIZATIONS

The phrases "defining moments" and "revealing, testing, and shaping" are brief and seem simple. Yet they are valuable guides for reflecting on personal decisions. In particular, they help people understand what is at stake when they must choose between right and right. These decisions compel people to reveal at least some of their basic values. They test how strongly individuals are committed to the values they espouse. And these decisions cast a shadow forward, shaping the rest of a person's life.

But managers cannot think in purely personal terms about the ethical dilemmas they face. In most cases, it would be naive, self-indulgent, and reckless for them to do so. For managers, defining moments are social as well as personal. Fortunately, the phrases "defining moments" and "revealing, testing, and shaping" are also powerful tools for understanding what right-versus-right decisions mean for an organization and what they mean for the managers who must make these decisions.

More importantly, the phrases call attention to one of the most challenging and creative elements of the work of business leaders: adapting, interpreting, and customizing basic human values in a way that guides and shapes an entire company. This is the task of shaping or creating a way of life, not for a person, but for an entire organization.

Defining moments for organizations, like those for individuals, can be subtle, quiet, and—examined one by one—seemingly inconsequential. Yet, whether managers intend it or not, their decisions and actions send continuous cumulative messages to their organizations about how things really work and about how to get ahead. Kremlinology—the intensive interpretation of all events, however minor, in the Soviet government—may be waning at the U.S. State Department now that the cold war is over, but it lives on in most companies. As one manager told me, "What many executives miss is that there is a very tight, silent, observational relationship between bosses and subordinates—because subordinates want to be promoted and get higher pay and status."

The Kremlinology intensifies when managers face right-versus-right issues. These differ from decisions about job assignments or budgeting, which everyone tries to decipher to get a sense of how the game is played and who is winning and losing. Right-versus-right issues differ in an important way: they offer everyone a glimpse at the ethical priorities of the people running a company, some clearer sense of what kind of people they really are.

These glimpses aren't merely a spectator sport; they influence how much trust people feel they can place in their bosses. Are they working for people who really care or who just pretend to care? Can we trust them when they say they back our project, like our work, or tell us that the layoffs are finally over?

At the organizational level, defining moments compel managers to reveal, test, and choose the ethics of their organization. Defining moments shape an organization because they cut through all of the finely crafted pronouncements about what the company aspires to do and reveal instead what it actually does. These episodes set precedents and create expectations that shape a company for years or even longer. They define the purpose of the organization and at the same time *how* the organization will pursue its purpose. Defining moments can matter as much to the life of an organization as they do to the life and career of a manager.

Defining moments also indelibly color the image that employees and others have of an organization and its leader. Clearly, defining moments are high-stakes episodes. At risk are not only a manager's personal commitments and values, but the character and morale of an organization as well. Stevens, for example, was the manager of a large domestic staff. There can be little doubt that the story of his choice on the final night of the conference was told and retold for years. Some members, perhaps many, were disappointed or repelled by what Stevens did. Nevertheless, he had set almost in stone an example of the commitments, values, and standards that would prevail at Darlington Hall.

Managers are the ethics teachers of their organizations. This is true whether they are saints or sinners, whether they intend to teach ethics or not. It simply comes with the territory. Actions send signals, and omissions send signals—almost everything does. Hence, responsible managers are concerned about their roles in the defining moments of their organizations. They care, that is, how their decisions and actions reveal, test, and shape the character of their companies.

This is why right-versus-right issues are defining moments. In these episodes, people define which moral values have the highest priority. They also define what these values mean in particular situations—for themselves and, if they are managers, for their organizations. That is the fundamental challenge that a defining moment can thrust into a manager's hands, often without advance notice.

Jean Paul Sartre, Chester Barnard, Aristotle, and John Dewey have helped us understand the nature of these problems. We will now turn to three other philosophers—Nietzsche, William James, and Machiavelli—for guidance on how to resolve them. They suggest important ways of reacting thoughtfully and responsibly to defining moments, and doing so as they arise.

The alternative is to look back on these choices, as Stevens did, with resignation and sorrow. His story raises troubling questions. Could Stevens have done better? Is there some way he could have understood, as he paused outside Miss Kenton's door, what was truly at stake? Are we, like him, condemned to brood over retrospective insights and to understand defining moments only after we can no longer change anything? Stevens did, after all, grasp something crucial about ethical choices: they can be turning points in a person's life. But he learned this much too late. The rest of this book proceeds on different assumptions: that thoughtful men and women can recognize defining moments as they happen, and that care and reflection matter greatly for resolving them well.

6

↔

Become Who You Are

THIS CHAPTER EXAMINES THE PERSONAL ASPECTS of the task of revealing, testing, and shaping. It asks what considerations are most important and what guidance seems most useful. This is a complicated subject. The best place to begin the search for answers is a relatively simple right-versus-right problem, like the one Steve Lewis, the apprentice investment banker, had to resolve. Recall his dilemma. He was asked, on very short notice, to attend an important client presentation. Although saying yes would help his firm and his career, Lewis was reluctant to go. The proposed assignment was purely decorative: his role at the meeting was to serve as an African-American potted plant.

Lewis faced a defining moment. His decision, whatever it was, would reveal something important about his character, values, and basic commitments in life. The situation would also test whatever values he had espoused in the past; he would now find out whether they were indeed *his* values or merely noble sentiments to which he had given lip service. Finally, his decisions and actions would shape his character, as well as his view of himself and the world— perhaps significantly. In essence, his choices would write a page of his moral autobiography.

Adario and Sakiz faced similar personal challenges. In their cases, however, the personal elements of their defining moments were intertwined with the important managerial aspects of their decisions. Adario's decision about Kathryn McNeil's schedule would reveal, test, and shape the values and norms of his department, while Sakiz's choices on RU 486 would compel him, under the glare of international media scrutiny, to define the role his firm would play in society and its relationships with major stakeholders. Nevertheless, both Adario and Sakiz would reveal which of their personal values and commitments stood at the head of the queue.

This chapter asks what advice and counsel pragmatic moralists offer to managers in situations like these. It presents their guidance in the form of four open-ended questions. Each of these includes a provocative phrase or refers to a thought-provoking passage. None offers a precise principle, a definitive answer, or an item on a checklist.

NIETZSCHE

A valuable way of understanding the personal aspects of right-versus-right problems originates from a seemingly unlikely source: the ideas of Friedrich Nietzsche. Nietzsche spent his entire career as a professor of classical literature; how could he have sound advice on real-world problems? He is also the reputed forerunner of Nazism and its horrors; how, then, could he provide ethical guidance? Clearly, before we turn to Nietzsche's ideas, we must examine his life.

He was born in Prussia in 1844, the son and grandson of ministers. A bookish, sensitive spirit, Nietzsche took up academic life and became a professor at the University of Basel in Switzerland when he was only 26. He spent the next 20 years writing prolifically, composing books, poems, journals, and brief essays. He also wrote countless aphorisms—short suggestive or provocative statements open to varied interpretations. Nietzsche's career ended when he went insane in 1889; he remained so until his death in 1900.

Nietzsche is most famous, or infamous, for a handful of aphorisms that proclaim the death of God. But his commanding intellectual stature derives from a host of startlingly original ideas about morality, individual and group psychology, power, and other basic facets of human life. Both critics and admirers regard Nietzsche as one of the most formidable thinkers of modern times. Indeed, Alasdair MacIntyre, one of the foremost contemporary interpreters of Aristotle, has written that "Nietzsche is *the* philosopher of the present age."[1] Nietzsche's literary skills are also extraordinary. He typically expresses himself in phrases so astute and well crafted that their force survives translation from German to English.

Was Nietzsche a Nazi? The answer is no. Until recently, his reputation has been the victim of his sister Elisabeth and her husband Bernard, a prominent anti-Semitic agitator. After his death, the two of them, along with several Nazi "intellectuals," scoured his publications and private notebooks, took a number of brief statements grossly out of context, and cobbled them together with the writings of others to create a pseudointellectual rationale for the Third Reich.

In reality, however, Nietzsche was repulsed by his brother-in-law's behavior. In a letter, he warned his sister not to connect him with her husband's work: "It is a matter of honor to me to be absolutely clean and unequivocal regarding anti-Semitism, namely opposed, as I am in my writings."[2] But, after his death, Nietzsche could no longer defend himself, and the efforts of modern scholars were needed to resurrect his reputation. They have demonstrated how vehemently he opposed racism, anti-Semitism, and German nationalism—the basic building blocks of Nazi ideology.[3] Nietzsche remains a controversial thinker, but the hostile takeover of his work by a few Nazi philosopher-quacks should not obscure his role in the development of Western thought, nor his usefulness for our purposes.[4]

NIETZSCHE AND ARISTOTLE

Nietzsche lived more than two millennia after Aristotle. The two men differed on a multitude of topics, but on at least one important topic their thoughts converged. Both viewed critical personal decisions, such as defining moments, not as single, separate events, but rather as the most recent link in the long chain of a person's past decisions, actions, and experiences. Nietzsche was particularly interested in another aspect of important decisions; they were also opportunities to forge the first link leading to a person's future.

Nietzsche describes the crux of the task in his recommendation to "Become who you are!"[5] At first, this advice may seem to bludgeon the obvious. Certainly, we need no effort to become ourselves, for that is what we already are. But Nietzsche had a clear agenda. He wanted his readers to pry themselves out of their familiar ways of thinking, avoid simplifying the complex, acknowledge with Aristotle that they are who they are, and yet remember the crucial, ongoing task of defining and refining their personalities and characters.

Nietzsche viewed people, potentially at least, as artists. What they create are their lives and their selves. The past is the raw material with which they must work. All this seems quite romantic—which is to say, hopelessly unrealistic and far removed from the daily life of business managers. But Nietzsche was no Pollyanna about the task of shaping or composing a life, especially given his view of the raw material—our pasts—with which we must work.

In *The Gay Science*, Nietzsche wrote:

To "give style" to one's character—a great and rare art! It is practiced by those who survey all the strengths and weaknesses of their nature and then fit them into an artistic plan until every one of them appears as art and reason and even weaknesses delight the eye. Here a large mass of second nature has been added; there a piece of original nature has been removed—both times through long practice and daily work at it. Here the ugly that could not be removed is concealed; there it has been reinterpreted and made sublime.[6]

Nietzsche described a person's past as a peculiar kind of raw material. A sculptor begins with a mass of soft clay that can be shaped into an endless variety of figures. Much of what a person works with is already formed and hardened. Some was shaped by other people, such as one's parents. Some of the preformed material is pleasing, some is awkward, some is plainly ugly. Hence, people need discipline, care, boldness, tenacity and single-mindedness, courage, and imagination to have any real chance of shaping their characters and becoming who they are.

This task is vitally important—particularly in defining moments, when people do, in some degree, shape themselves. Nietzsche believed that people who ignore this task end up living lives designed by others or generic lives selected from the shelf of mass culture. To drive home his point, he calls these people "the herd." He asks, in effect: Why be a commodity? Why not create and live a life of your own?

Recall the regrets of the butler Stevens about the life he might have led with Miss Kenton, but didn't, or the intense pressures on Lewis, Adario, and Sakiz. At times, many managers feel that their friends and families have become impediments to the smooth functioning of the modern economy. In contexts like these, the ancient Greek admonition to know oneself, and Nietzsche's modern version of it—to become who you are—seem especially daunting projects.

But how can Nietzsche's advice be translated into practice? In the midst of a defining moment and a hard choice among conflicting responsibilities, what does it mean to "become who you are"? Four questions provide specific guidance.

THE HEART'S REASONS

The first question is: How do my feelings and intuitions define, for me, the right-versus-right conflict? Answering this question is the first step in making use of the advice to become who you are. This step is a matter of asking just what the problem seems to be—not in objective terms that hold true for everyone, but for a particular individual, with his or her own hopes and fears, values, and experiences. In short, the first question doesn't simply ask how you feel. It asks what your feelings tell you.

Steve Lewis, as we have seen, was uncomfortable and anxious about the St. Louis presentation. But his instincts did more than sound an alarm; they also gave an initial sense of what was at stake. Basically, Lewis felt that the St. Louis trip pitted self-respect against loyalty. Although he could think of many counterarguments and other ways of looking at the situation, this was what his intuition told him.

"Almost every racial dilemma I had confronted," Lewis later recalled, "involved the recognition of achievement rather than blatant rejection due to race." His response to these situations was a personal philosophy that he summarized as "Action over words." He had always chosen to take advantage of the opportunities offered him, rather than stew over why he was offered them. He knew he had earned or overearned his opportunities, but instead of trying to explain this to others, his aim was to show them that he deserved the opportunities and would make the most of them.

In the past, however, Lewis knew he had earned the awards and was qualified to meet the challenges of the opportunities offered him. That didn't seem to be the case now. The St. Louis "opportunity" was last-minute, he hadn't worked on the project, and his only role was to show up. "Action over words" didn't seem to justify joining the presentation. At the same time, he wanted to be a team player and not disappoint his mentor, friends, and superiors. Lewis was an active athlete in high school and college intramural sports. Although he was no star, he prided himself on his team spirit.

Notice how Lewis used his feelings of discomfort and anxiety. He didn't try to sense which feelings were strongest and then do whatever would leave him feeling less bad. He used them to gain an initial intuition that the heart of the conflict, at least for him, was between self-respect and loyalty.

Lewis was, in effect, following an approach suggested by Blaise Pascal, the French mathematician and philosopher of the seventeenth century. In *Pensées*, his extended defense of Christianity, Pascal makes a famous observation. "The heart," he writes, "has its reasons that reason does not know."

Note Pascal's belief, and Aristotle's as well, that the heart offers more than simply feelings or inchoate impulses. Emotions do more than indicate crudely and vividly that something feels good or bad. A person's feelings can actually help make sense of an issue, give shape to it, and indicate what the stakes really are. In other words, the heart has *reasons*.

But these reasons are written in a language different from the formal, explicit, logical one with which our minds operate. Discerning how one's instincts define a situation is a matter of translation. It is an interpretive art, and a difficult one. Professional translators sometimes cite the warning "Translator. Traitor." By the same token, not everything that is compressed or expressed in a feeling or intuition can be translated into precise, objective terms. There is a risk of betrayal. Indeed, Pascal's famous adage can be read to suggest that reason simply cannot understand all of the heart's reasons.

Nevertheless, effort like the one Steve Lewis made—to articulate, as well as he could, his personal sense of what was at stake—can be a valuable first step in applying the advice "Become who you are."

THE ROOTS OF RESPONSIBILITY

Instinct had now served its role as an initial guide to Lewis's decision. He had a definite sense of which of his values, commitments, and responsibilities were in conflict. Now he needed further guidance.

Following the advice "Become who you are" involves learning who one has been. This means answering a second basic question: How deep are the moral roots of the conflicting values that are creating the right-versus-right conflict? Tracing the "roots" of one's values means understanding their origins, evolution, and importance in a person's life. It involves an effort to understand which values and commitments really have, up to the present, defined a person's moral identity.

Sophocles' great drama *Antigone*, written not long before Aristotle's birth, illustrates what it means to trace the personal and social roots of ethical responsibilities. In the play, Antigone must make a tragic choice. A bloody civil war has just ended, and one of her brothers has been declared a traitor. The king has ordered that his body be left unburied, "to be eaten," in Sophocles' words, "by dogs and vultures, a horror for all to see."[7] Antigone must decide whether to obey the royal edict or to give her brother a proper burial and risk death by stoning.

At the cost of her life, Antigone chooses the latter. The play shows the powerful emotions that drive her choice—at one point, she declares her hatred for her sister, who chooses not to break the law. But, for Antigone, intuition isn't a matter of passionate, inexplicable emotion. Throughout the play, she strives to explain her decision—to her sister, to the king, and to herself. The deep roots of her choice gradually become clear. They lie in her understanding of the "holiest laws of the heavens," the "high blood" that flows in her veins and her sense of honor, her devotion to her family, the belief that she is atoning for the awful deeds of her father, Oedipus, and carrying "the unending burden" of her family heritage.

Antigone's conviction that she must bury her brother is a compelling personal truth. Her commitment expresses and reflects the abiding commitments of her life and experience, and those of her family. Few ethical dilemmas are as momentous as Antigone's, but they are nevertheless opportunities for people to understand themselves more deeply. The task is to place the problem at hand in the context of earlier defining moments in one's life. The challenge, in Marcel Proust's phrase, is to become a "reader of yourself."

By looking back across a series of these defining episodes, people can begin to see patterns of ethical commitments and interpretations that are distinctively their own. Williams James revered these past episodes, calling them "the workshop of being." In the last chapter of *Pragmatism*, he writes, "Our acts, our turning-places, where we seem to ourselves to make ourselves and grow, are the parts of the world to which we are the closest, the parts of which our knowledge is the most intimate and complete."[8]

Steve Lewis's challenge was to try to understand which side of his dilemma had the deepest roots in his life. Although he had little time for reflection, he soon found himself thinking of earlier situations in his life when he had been singled out because of his race. These were, in effect, early defining moments, which he interpreted through his personal credo "Action over words."

Although all these moments were personal, they also reflected his family's experiences. Among these, one incident stood out. In the early 1960s, his parents made a reservation at a restaurant that reputedly did not serve blacks. When they arrived, the hostess told them there had been a mistake, the reservation was lost, and they could not be seated, even though the restaurant was half empty. Lewis's parents turned around and left. When they got home, his mother made a new reservation under her maiden name. The restaurant suspected nothing. When they returned there an hour later, the hostess, though hardly overjoyed, proceeded to seat them.

Events like these mean different things to different people, but what was important for Lewis is what they meant to him, in the few minutes available to make a decision. Steve Lewis was galvanized when he thought about what his parents had done. Even now, years after the events, he felt angry, humiliated, and proud. Although he had no time to finish his list of pros and cons, he sensed and felt what seemed right. He would view the situation as his parents' son. He would also view it as an African American, not as just another young investment banker. And he could not go to the meeting as the token black, because this would repudiate his parents' example. He had decided, in effect, that this was a vital part of his moral identity, one with deeper and more complex connections to his past life than the professional role he had recently assumed.

Lewis had clarified his moral starting point. The philosopher Alasdair MacIntyre describes this perspective in these terms:

> *I am someone's son or daughter, someone else's cousin or uncle; I am a citizen of this or that city, a member of this or that guild or profession; I belong to this tribe, that clan, this nation. I inherit from the past of my family, my city, my tribe, my nation, a variety of debts, inheritances, rightful expectations and obligations. These constitute the given of my life, my moral starting point. This is in part what gives my life its own moral particularity.*[9]

Lewis had now made some progress. He had defined the basic conflict in terms of his personal values and responsibilities. He believed he knew which of these were connected most strongly to his past life. But were these the values by which he wanted to shape his future? This question remained unanswered. So, too, did the question of just what he should do; Lewis still lacked a plan of action.

THIS IS *MY* WAY; WHERE IS YOURS?

Antigone's story is inspiring. At the cost of her life, she upholds the commitments and values that define her moral identity. At the same time, because of its dire conclusion, her story is deeply troubling. Creon, the king whose edict she disobeys, also remains faithful to his responsibilities. As the new ruler of a community torn by civil war, his foremost aims are to restore order and prop up the fragile authority of the government. Like Antigone, Creon will not bend. He sentences her to death, her fiancé—his son—commits suicide, and these horrors impel Creon's wife to kill herself.

Was Antigone a martyr to her values, or their victim? She remained faithful to her family and her past, as she interpreted them, but her devotion doomed her to relive their awful fate. This suggests that, on some occasions, it may be *irresponsible* to let the commitments and ideals of the past, however deep and complex their moral roots, become the prologue and pilot for the future. Becoming who you are also involves choosing which of your abiding instincts and commitments you will leave alone and which you will struggle to reshape.

In 1990, the American writer Calvin Trillin wrote a brief account of the life of a college friend, Roger "Denny" Hansen. Denny graduated from Yale in 1957, where he seemed to stand head and shoulders above his classmates. He had a powerful mind, a luminous smile, and brilliant prospects in life. Trillin says he was "stunningly complete." In fact, Denny's college friends occasionally played a game in which they guessed what positions they would hold in President Roger Hansen's cabinet.

Unfortunately, the game was horribly misguided. Denny never sought elective office. In his later years, Trillin writes, he "didn't look as if he had any smiles in him." And, at the age of 55, Hansen locked himself in an acquaintance's garage, started a car engine, and let carbon monoxide take his life.

Trillin's book, *Remembering Denny*, sets out to explain how the splendid youth known as Denny evolved into the ailing, almost-friendless, and despondent man whom acquaintances called Roger. A woman who knew Hansen looked at his death this way: "The way I see promise is that you have a knapsack, and all the time you're growing up they keep stuffing promise into the knapsack." She added, "Pretty soon, it's just too heavy to carry. You have to unpack."[10]

The task, of course, isn't so simple. As Aristotle and Nietzsche emphasize, people cannot pack and unpack their knapsacks as easily as the metaphor suggests. We often deny or repress what we are carrying around, despite good faith efforts to understand ourselves.

Nevertheless, had Denny looked into his knapsack, he would have found a set of clear expectations about the right way—the morally valid way—for him to live his life. "Roles were set," Trillin writes, "and set for life." Some of these expectations were Denny's own, some originated with the friends who adulated him in high school and college, and some were 1950s notions of what defined a decent, responsible life for someone with his background. He was expected to complete his Rhodes scholarship at Oxford, graduate from a first-class law school, get married somewhere along the way, and then begin his political ascent.

The weight of these expectations eventually crushed Denny, for the right life for him was very different. He wanted to work as a scholar and a teacher, which he ultimately did. He wanted friends who accepted him for what he was, rather than for what they needed him to be. This he may never have accomplished. Above all, perhaps, he wanted a partner in life—specifically, a male partner. For, while everyone around him seemed to assume that Denny was heterosexual and that homosexuality was a psychological abnormality and a personal failure, Roger understood that he was gay.

Hansen struggled for most of his adult life to answer a question that Nietzsche posed in *Thus Spake Zarathustra*. It is also the third basic question for sorting out the personal meaning of right-versus-right decisions. At one point, Zarathustra says, " 'This is *my* way; where is yours?'—thus I answered those who asked me 'the way.' For *the* way—that does not exist."[11] Although she sacrificed her life, Antigone may well have chosen her "way" and embraced her fate—the play leaves this somewhat unclear. But Roger Hansen struggled at the task for most of his life.

What do Nietzsche's views of ethics suggest for people who, like Steve Lewis, face difficult issues of moral identity? Nietzsche's basic question—What is your way?—urges people to look at critical choices, not simply as the culmination of their pasts, but as the first steps in the shaping of their future selves. The point is to look down the road and not only through the rear-view mirror.

Nietzsche is emphatic on this point. He wants to help people escape from "the musty agreeable nooks into which preference and prejudice, youth, origin, the accidents of people and books or even exhaustion from wandering seem to have abandoned us."[12] Nietzsche warns vigorously against defining a problem in terms of values that one hasn't embraced for oneself. People may, at times, need to be *untrue* to themselves—if their selves consist too much of others' values.

Steve Lewis believed he was pursuing his own values in seeking to become a partner at a Wall Street investment bank. This was the life he wanted to live and a kind of work he knew he would enjoy doing. Moreover, this was an abiding dream and hardly a passing fancy. Since his sophomore year of college, Lewis had been fascinated by the idea of a career on Wall Street, and he had worked hard and purposefully to make it possible.

When he accepted his current job, he had finally set foot on the path he had dreamed of for so long, and neither the long hours nor the detailed grunt work, which was the lot of first-year analysts, gave him misgivings about his choice. He loved the competitive, fast-paced world he had entered. Moreover, Lewis had little doubt that the dream was his—if anything, his parents were concerned about his career choice. They didn't think Wall Street was the most welcoming environment for a young African American. But this made the challenge even more compelling for Lewis. Moreover, even though he knew that his strongest motives were personal, he realized that his success would help open doors for others.

To the question What is your way? Lewis had a firm answer. He had no doubt that he wanted to become a partner at a major investment bank. This realization intensified Lewis's dilemma and clarified how high the stakes were for him. He would not betray his parents' example, nor his personal interpretation of it: "Action over words." These defined much of who he was. At the same time, he did not want to imperil a job and a career that defined much of what he hoped to become.

SEEING THE WORLD AS IT IS

Another important moralist, Niccolo Machiavelli, has thus far been silent. But, of course, this should surprise no one. Neither the evolution of moral identity, nor the roots of ethical responsibilities, nor the morality of aspirations were among his paramount concerns.

Machiavelli would have much to say to Steve Lewis. However, as with Nietzsche, there is the question of whether Lewis should listen to him. Machiavelli is, after all, the alleged high priest of untrammeled self-interest, duplicity, and the poisoned chalice. But would Machiavelli be known to the world today if he were simply the first to argue that sleazy people sometimes get ahead? Would hundreds of books and articles still examine his ideas if he simply advocated craftiness as a political tactic? The ancient Greeks understood the occasional utility of deception, as did the Israelites, and the Romans, and as does every three-year-old child. Surely, Machiavelli must have had something complex and important to say about leadership, power, and the ethics of real-world decisions.

For him, ethics and politics were matters of practical knowledge and wisdom derived from hands-on experience. Machiavelli lived in Florence from 1469 to 1527, amid the artistic grandeur, intellectual ferment, and political turbulence of the Renaissance. He was a close observer of politics—as an insider working at the highest levels of Florence's government, as an outsider sent into exile by the Medicis, and as an avid student of political history.

Machiavelli believed, above all else, that successful leaders must see the world as it really is. Chapter after chapter of *The Prince*, his masterwork, combines his analysis with examples of how successful leaders actually behaved. The book is full of phrases like "putting aside imaginary things," "our experience has been," and "endless modern examples could be given."

If Machiavelli were looking over Steve Lewis's shoulder, he would likely tell him that his reflections and aspirations, however heartfelt, were the mere gossamer of youthful idealism. Machiavelli would call his attention to the hard realities of his situation, particularly the force field of power and self-interest in which Lewis found himself. At best, Lewis had a single, minor bargaining chip: he could create a temporarily awkward situation, essentially an inconvenience, by saying no to the St. Louis presentation.

Playing this chip, however, was risky. The word on the street was that reputations were formed very early at his firm. The grapevine let the organization know who could make their numbers, who the team players were, and who really belonged on the fast track. Lewis had already heard from a second-year analyst what happened when he failed to "go along with the program." The person's boss "started treating other people better. He wasn't on my side anymore, and you needed him on your side to do things. He wasn't my buddy anymore. It made it really difficult to get the kind of support you needed to be a top performer."

Machiavelli would quickly recognize the affirmative action game that the firm and its client were playing. Lewis was in the right place, at the right time, with the right skin color. If the client had been a white Yale graduate who loved golf, the firm would have sent one of its Yale golfers. But the game was a little tricky, perhaps even perilous, and Machiavelli would surely want Lewis to tally the risks and rewards.

Attending the meeting would let Lewis log some valuable "face time" with his bosses on the plane flight and before and after the meeting. He might improve his professional skills by watching the presentation. And, if his firm were chosen, Lewis could bask in the glow of success and perhaps even participate in follow-up work for the client.

But what if Lewis was embarrassed at the St. Louis meeting? He knew nothing about the project, which involved a highly specialized area of municipal finance. What if someone at the presentation asked him what part of the project he worked on or asked him a technical question about the deal? Would he bluff? What if he got in over his head and imperiled the deal? Another risk was resentment among the analysts and associates who were passed over even though they knew more about municipal finance. His firm was intensely competitive; would they try to trip him up later? In short, what little power Lewis had was awkward for him to use.

The Prince is Machiavelli's advice to leaders on recognizing the realities of their situation and ways to gain, keep, and use power. Much of his guidance rests on this observation:

how one lives is so far distant from how one ought to live, that he who neglects what is done for what ought to be done, sooner effects his ruin than his preservation; for a man who wishes to act entirely up to his professions of virtue soon meets with what destroys him among so much that is evil.

In short, if ethics is not practical, it is little more than greeting-card sentiment, and it can be downright dangerous. Lewis—and others similarly situated—should never stray too far from Machiavelli's fundamental question: What will work in the world as it is?

This question can easily be misunderstood, however, and Machiavelli would have insisted on two qualifications. First, he did not intend to endorse or praise slippery, sleazy, or immoral behavior. He acknowledged that such behavior was wrong and dangerous. (Indeed, much of *The Prince* describes ways to conceal such behavior.) The essential point about trickery and subterfuge is not that they are the first choice or the last choice; rather, in some circumstances, they are simply the necessary choice, in the world as we find it.

Machiavelli's perspective is echoed in the personal "survival principles" a manager once described to me: "Do what is necessary to protect yourself, even if this involves some moral compromise; see things as they are in order to be successful; keep your passions under control and be objective; pick your battles carefully." Like Machiavelli, this manager did not embrace immorality for immorality's sake. She simply acknowledged what is sometimes necessary in an intensely competitive and sometimes unscrupulous world.

Machiavelli's second qualification would be this: he did not intend to endorse or praise timidity, short-sightedness, business as usual, or the easy way out. He admired boldness, as long as shrewdness guided it. Fortune, he believed, could best be taken by storm. Hence, if Machiavelli were counseling Steve Lewis, his basic question would be: What combination of expediency and shrewdness, coupled with imagination and boldness, will move you closer to your personal goals?

WIGGLE ROOM

Where do the ideas of Aristotle, Nietzsche, and Machiavelli leave Steve Lewis? Certainly not with a formula or a grand principle for deciding what to do. Perhaps with a clearer sense of the personal stakes in this decision—the ways this decision will reveal, test, and shape his values and character. Perhaps also with an awareness of the importance of four questions: How do my feelings and instincts define the dilemma? Which of the responsibilities and values in conflict have the deepest roots in my life and in communities I care about? Looking to the future, what is *my* way? And how can expediency and shrewdness, along with imagination and boldness, move me toward the goals I care about most strongly?

These questions can also serve as practical criteria for devising a plan of action. Notice how the questions balance each other and limit the risks that each one, considered alone, might create. Taken by itself, for example, Machiavelli's question could lead someone like Lewis to focus too heavily on what is expedient in the present moment. This tendency is balanced by Aristotle's emphasis on the roots of one's responsibilities in one's life and community, and by Nietzsche's question—What is *your* way?—which draws attention to the future.

Lewis's basic task was one that thoughtful people often face: pursuing the morally laudable quest for "wiggle room." He needed to find a plan of action that would preserve the values he cared about without making him a noble, young, unnoticed martyr. Lewis decided to join the presentation team, but he also gambled that he could do so on terms that were at least acceptable to him. He told his colleagues that he felt honored to be asked but added that he wanted to play a role in the presentation. He said he was willing to spend every minute of the next 30 hours in preparation. When he was asked why this mattered, Lewis said nothing about how he was chosen, his reluctance to be used as a token black, or his personal philosophy of "Action over words." All he said was that he wanted to earn his place on the team.

Lewis's colleagues reluctantly agreed. There was, it turned out, a minor element of the presentation that required the application of some basic analytical techniques with which Lewis had worked. When Lewis stood up for the 12 minutes allotted him, he had a terrible headache and wished he had simply said no to the offer. His single day of cramming was no substitute for the weeks his colleagues had invested in the project. But, though he couldn't recall it very clearly, his presentation apparently went well enough. He finally began to relax when he realized that no one had questions for him.

On the flight back, Lewis's colleagues thanked him for helping out, especially on short notice. They never said anything about why Lewis had been chosen, and during the next few weeks no one said anything more about what he had done. Lewis was invited to the small party that was held when his firm was awarded the work.

On balance, Lewis was pleased and relieved about what he had done. He believed he had defined the dilemma soundly, at least in terms of his experiences and values. And, on the whole, he resolved it without betraying his parents and himself by merely attending the meeting and serving a decorative function. At the same time, his career prospects may have been strengthened. He felt he had passed a minor test, a rite of passage at his firm, and demonstrated that he was willing to do what it took to get the job done. The white analysts and associates who were passed over probably did some grumbling, but Lewis suspected that, if they had been dealt his hand, they would have played their cards as he did.

Perhaps Lewis's hands were a little dirty. He hadn't told his colleagues what he really thought, and he did participate in a charade, suggesting to the client that he had played a larger role than he actually did. And, from Aristotle's perspective, he may have begun a habit of compromising his values in order to climb the greasy pole. This habit could someday culminate in a serious betrayal of his values. At times, Lewis wished he had said something or stood up for his beliefs—and he hoped that he would do so on future occasions, once he had established himself. But, to do this, he felt he had to pick his battles. As Machiavelli observed, "A man who has no position in life cannot even get a dog to bark at him."

As for Nietzsche's injunction, "Become who you are," Lewis hoped he had taken a small step toward becoming, in the phrase of one of his college teachers, an "ethically sensitive pragmatist." Surely he had been pragmatic, as he and his parents had been in the past. He hoped that, at the same time, he had honored the values by which he hoped to shape his life.

Only time would reveal the importance of this defining moment in Steve Lewis's early professional years. But if his career prospered, this episode was much more likely to become a paragraph, rather than a full chapter, in his permanent moral record. If Lewis eventually achieved real managerial responsibilities, his decisions would then affect hundreds, perhaps thousands of other people. However difficult this episode seemed as it unfolded, defining moments like those facing Peter Adario and Edouard Sakiz would prove to be much more challenging.

7

↔

Truth Is a Process

T HIS CHAPTER EXAMINES DEFINING MOMENTS for organizations. It presents guidance for managers who want to handle these situations practically and responsibly. Before turning to this guidance, however, it is important to know what happened to Peter Adario when he tried to resolve the issue of Kathryn McNeil's schedule.

Remember that Adario viewed this as an ethical issue, a conflict of right versus right. As a manager, he was pulled in two directions. Some of his responsibilities and values led him to conclude that it would be wrong to fire McNeil. Others told him she had to be replaced because her work was falling behind schedule. The problem required immediate attention, because Lisa Walters was pressuring Adario to fire McNeil. Adario also needed a creative solution, because there were no spare funds to hire another assistant for McNeil and no way to reassign her.

Adario got a large cup of coffee, closed his door, and resolved to find an answer before turning to his other work for the day. He soon found himself thinking about a case study from his MBA days, 12 years earlier. It described the 1982 decision by James Burke, the chairman of Johnson & Johnson, to pull all containers of Tylenol capsules, with a retail value of $100 million, from the nation's shelves, after six people in the Chicago area died from taking poisoned Tylenol capsules. Burke's decision was a defining moment for Johnson & Johnson. It revealed, tested, and renewed the company's commitment to its ethical values and its corporate credo.

Adario admired Burke's decision and wanted to follow his example, albeit on a modest scale. Specifically, he hoped to use the McNeil issue to send two clear messages. He wanted to show the managers working for him how difficult decisions could be made with more thought and sensitivity, instead of the bulldozing style prevalent at Sayer MicroWorld. He was also eager to take a tangible step in the direction of a family-friendly workplace.

By the time Adario finished his coffee, he had a plan. He would arrange to meet with Walters and McNeil in the next day or two and tell them to hammer out an agreement before the end of the meeting. If that failed, Adario would step in with suggestions. McNeil's work had to get done and done on time—the IBM account was simply too important. But perhaps McNeil could take some work home or telecommute; perhaps she could work all day, every other Saturday; perhaps, he hoped, the real issue was some misunderstanding between the two women, which the company's pressure-cooker atmosphere had intensified. Perhaps all they needed was a chance to vent their feelings and hear each other's concerns.

Adario sent email messages to Walters and McNeil and then left his office to make a presentation at a trade show. As he drove away, Adario felt good about his plan. In personal terms, he was pleased he wasn't taking the easy way out. Unlike the boss who had fired his next-door neighbor, Adario was going the extra mile to save McNeil's job. He also felt he was standing up for some of his basic values, such as treating people decently, and was even doing something for McNeil's son. He looked forward to telling his wife what he had done.

Adario also thought his plan made good managerial sense. By letting Walters and McNeil work out a solution, he would avoid being heavy-handed or manipulative—they would "own" their plan, thereby making it more likely to succeed. By getting personally involved and helping McNeil, Adario was showing that he cared about the people in his unit. And, in his mind, the tactic of keeping everyone at the table until they had all agreed on a plan would remind everyone of the urgency of the company's situation.

Adario's presentation went well, as did a long lunch meeting with an important retailer. For the first time in several weeks, Adario was having a good day, and he felt he deserved it. Even the paperwork waiting on his desk didn't dismay him. Unfortunately, however, as soon as he returned to his office, he learned that McNeil had been fired.

Walters, it turned out, had been discussing the situation with several other managers, including a senior vice president, who had offered to help her fire McNeil. When McNeil walked into her office early that afternoon, she found Walters and the vice president waiting for her. They immediately handed her a letter of termination, which said she was not "a good fit with the management staff." McNeil was told to spend the rest of the afternoon bringing her replacement up to speed. (Walters had reassigned someone from another area and also volunteered to help out.) McNeil was told to collect her last paycheck and two weeks of severance pay, pack her personal belongings, turn in her ID badge, and leave the premises.

This episode had become a defining moment for Adario's unit, but hardly the one he had planned. Two signals had been sent: one clear and one garbled. The clear message was "Families are an impediment to the efficient operation of this company." The other message was either "It's okay to go around your boss" or "It's okay to go around Adario." Faced with a right-versus-right choice, he had ended up with neither "right." His intentions were admirable, but his effort to shape his organization's values had gone badly awry.

Adario had started out well. He recognized that this episode could be a defining moment for his organization and that it could provide part of the answer to the questions Who are we? and What do we stand for? Adario was also thinking in practical terms—about the values he wanted to guide his department and the messages that his decisions and actions might send.

But events turned out badly. The reason, in part, was that Adario drew the wrong lessons—simple, inspirational, "do-the-right-thing" lessons—from the Tylenol episode. As a result, he overestimated the role of good intentions and lofty ethical sentiments in defining moments. He also underestimated the role of management skill and effort, as well as shrewdness and street smarts. He thought he could accomplish, in one fell swoop, a task that demanded months of astute effort.

Adario also failed to think through his answers to four questions that the ethical realists might have posed, questions that can raise the odds that managers will succeed in using important decisions as defining moments for their organizations. Had Adario addressed these questions, he would also have understood why the task of defining or redefining an organization's values is one of the most subtle and demanding challenges of managerial work.

THE CONTEST OF INTERPRETATIONS

Some of the most valuable, down-to-earth guidance for Peter Adario would have come from an unlikely source, a man who was born into a literary family, spent his entire career as a Harvard professor, never managed a company, never wrote about business, and dismissed the world of commerce as "mere trade."[1] That man is William James. Trained as a medical doctor, he became renowned as a psychologist, a student of religion, and a philosopher. Indeed, he helped found and popularize the school of thought called pragmatism. And it is James's pragmatic, psychologically realistic way of thinking about the age-old question What is truth? that is exceedingly relevant to managers like Peter Adario.

In his book *Pragmatism*, William James uses a peculiar phrase to summarize the first lesson Adario needed to learn. There he wrote, "The trail of the human serpent is thus over everything."[2] James believed there was no such thing as "Truth independent; truth that we *find* merely; truth no longer malleable to human need."[3] At first glance, this sounds like an idea that is at once both silly and danger-ous. It seems to dismiss even the possibility of truth, thereby discarding reality, science, and objectivity. At the same time, James's idea threatens to open the door to madmen and tyrants, who will define truth in whatever way pleases them. But none of this is what sober, serious, practical-minded William James had in mind. In playing down "the facts" and stressing the malleability of "the truth," he was arguing that we inevitably see "the facts" through our interpretive lenses.

Recall Antigone and Creon. Both were citizens of the same city, both knew its laws and religion, both had lived through the same bloody civil war. Yet they interpreted the shared facts of their community and its religious life in diametrically and tragically different ways. Recall the butler Stevens. He viewed his master as a high-minded diplomat, as did many political leaders; others saw only a Nazi dupe. Consider our daily experience. Companies regularly release financial data, accompanied by their interpretation of it, and then financial analysts develop their own interpretations of whether companies are really doing well or not. Politicians compete at "spin," and we interpret their interpretations. And, of course, Peter Adario and Lisa Walters looked at the same facts about Kathryn McNeil and reached very different conclusions.

The point is not that facts do not matter, or that nothing is true or false. The German writer Goethe wrote that "Experience is only half of experience." The other half is the multitude of ways in which people perceive, weight, simplify, and explain experience—in a word, how they interpret it. Of course, there are facts and they matter, but we surround them, overlay them, and suffuse them with interpretation. "All our formulas," James writes, "have a human twist."[4]

The conventional wisdom about Johnson & Johnson and the 1982 Tylenol episode is a triumph of interpretation. For 15 years, Johnson & Johnson has reposed on a pedestal, in the media and in business ethics classrooms, as a result of the Tylenol episode. But this was hardly inevitable, for the story of Johnson & Johnson, its credo, and its values lends itself to more than one interpretation.

In the early 1980s, for example, the company was widely criticized for its delay in recalling its highly successful painkiller Zomax, which was implicated in at least 14 deaths. One of Johnson & Johnson's directors of regulatory affairs commented, "We resisted too much and waited too long." Where, one might ask, was the company credo? More than 800 product liability suits were filed over Zomax, and by 1988 all but 3 had been settled out of court. The settlements included provisions that barred the plaintiffs from revealing what they had learned about the drug.[5]

In 1986, a second Tylenol episode took place. It, too, cost a human life, because someone penetrated the triple-protective seal Johnson & Johnson had introduced after the six deaths from poisoned Tylenol in 1982. In other words, it took yet another death to induce the company to stop selling capsule products over the counter. Was the company's first response to the first death a case of "too little, too late"?

In 1990, Johnson & Johnson introduced a new fiberglass cast, using technology that a court concluded was stolen from 3M. A judge in the ensuing litigation ordered the company to pay $116 million for patent infringement and misappropriation of trade secrets.[6] A few years later, Johnson & Johnson was fined $7.5 million for shredding documents and otherwise obstructing a federal agency that was investigating charges that, for years, Johnson & Johnson had illegally marketed one of its drugs.[7]

It is easy to imagine an alternative interpretation of Johnson & Johnson's recent history. Its centerpiece would be Zomax, not Tylenol, because the Zomax episode was the first of a series of incidents in which the company seemed to ignore its credo. The famous Tylenol episode, from this perspective, is the exception—and a rather feeble one—that proves the rule. That is, the decision to pull the product can be viewed as a no-brainer. National news broadcasts about the six deaths had instilled almost-universal fear of Tylenol, Johnson & Johnson's reputation was in peril, and the financial cost of pulling the product was far less than $100 million, because few consumers wanted to play Russian roulette to cure their headaches.

What, then, is the "truth independent" about the Tylenol episode and Johnson & Johnson's commitment to its credo? Why did one interpretation of the company and its values triumph over the others? James Burke gave part of the answer when he said that, during the 1982 Tylenol episode, the media became, in his phrase, the company's "handmaiden." This was hardly an accident. Instead, as we will see, it is compelling testimony to Burke's management skills, values, experience, tenacity, shrewdness, and tactical instincts. As a result, the Tylenol story became a defining moment, revealing and renewing the company's commitment to the important human values in its credo. One interpretation among many had won the contest of interpretations.

Had Adario understood this, his chances of success would have been considerably higher. He acted as if his personal view of the ethics of the Kathryn McNeil situation were the objective truth, rather than his interpretation. For example, where Adario saw right versus right, Lisa Walters saw right versus wrong. She believed that the basic ethical issue was responsibility—or, more precisely, McNeil's irresponsibility for not pulling her weight and Adario's irresponsibility for not taking action. The IBM account was crucial, and it was falling behind schedule during a period of near-crisis for the company. Walters also believed it was unfair for one member of the badly overburdened team to get special treatment.

Had Peter Adario recognized that his view was just one interpretation among many, he might have proceeded more successfully. Once Adario was clear about the values he wanted to encourage in his department, he should have asked himself the first of four important questions: What are the other strong, persuasive, competing interpretations of the situation or problem that I hope to use as a defining moment for my organization?

The answer to this question might have been a wake-up call for Adario. It might have helped him to abandon his lofty view of events and realize that he was engaged in a difficult contest of interpretations, not a righteous quest for truth and goodness. Peter Adario's "family-friendly" cooperative worldview was vying against Lisa Walter's competitive, "Let's give it all we've got and save the company" ethos.

Truth "Works"

What kind of interpretation is most likely to win a contest of interpretation inside an organization and influence the thinking and behavior of other people? William James gives a complex and subtle answer to this question, an answer that managers like Peter Adario need to understand if they want to succeed in getting particular ideas, interpretations, and values to become "true" for their organizations.

For James, successful ideas, victorious ideas, are the ideas that work. This may sound simple, but it is actually a complicated and unusual way of thinking about truth. The conventional view of truth is much simpler. It holds that a statement is true if it corresponds to some external reality. For example, the statement "That bug is dead" is true if someone makes it about a dead bug. In other words, a true statement is like a mirror held up to reality.

This approach to truth runs into serious difficulties, James believed, when we are dealing with complex, important matters such as ethics or religion. Our experience continues to matter critically, but not in a simple, mirror-of-reality, dead-bug way. Ideas become true, James writes, when they work, when they meet real humans' needs and pass the test of lived experience.

Put more formally, true ideas have three characteristics. First, they have "cash-value in experiential terms" and are "profitable to our lives."[8] Second, they can also be grafted onto ideas we already hold to be true, without causing much disturbance. Third, true ideas are down to earth, not esoteric. "The finally victorious way of looking at things," he writes, "will be the most completely *impressive* to the normal run of minds."[9]

What does this way of thinking imply for managers? Had Peter Adario thought in these terms, he would have worked hard to find ways of presenting his view of work-family issues in ways that might have proven valuable in the immediate experience of others, that would disturb their worldviews as little as possible, and that they could hear and understand in simple English. This might have meant changing the way he phrased the issue. "Work-family" meant roughly the same thing to Adario, to his wife, and to McNeil. Its meaning was their constant fatigue, their everyday sense of being pulled in a thousand directions, and the frustration of never catching up on all they had to do. For them, this was what James would call the cash-value, stream-of-experience meaning of work-family issues.

In contrast, the phrase meant little, in experiential terms, to most of the other employees at Sayer MicroWorld. Few were parents, almost all were young and single. In their everyday stream of experience, however, the cash-value meaning of "work-family" was that they sometimes had to work longer hours because other employees with children had left for soccer games or doctor's appointments. Had Adario used phrases like "a balanced life" or "time for recharging one's batteries" as a way of describing and interpreting the values he wanted his department to follow, he would have had some prospect of grafting his ideas onto the views and experiences of other employees.

For Adario's boss, the vice president who was preoccupied with cash flow and operating performance, "work-family" was a red flag. It smacked of political correctness, promised more task forces and policy statements, and threatened to raise costs and make his job more complicated. For Adario's hopes to have any chance of success, he needed convincing ways of describing his agenda in terms of raising productivity or improving recruiting. An interpretation is much more likely to succeed and become the truth for a company if it makes the business stronger or meets the needs of the people running it.

These suggestions for Adario can easily be misunderstood. They may look like verbal sleight of hand, clever sound bites, or political propaganda. Although it is true that ethics must often sneak in the back door of a company or cross-dress as economics and self-interest, James isn't recommending devious tactics. He is calling for acts of creativity, insight, and skill that enable a manager like Peter Adario to express ideals and values in ways that resonate with the experience, needs, and values of the people he manages. This requires a talent for looking beyond "the facts" and discerning what they *mean* to other people.

James Burke, with his long and successful experience in marketing, relied on this talent in a crucial early moment of the 1982 Tylenol episode. Some managers at Johnson & Johnson argued that the company faced a "Tylenol problem"—a business problem affecting a single product. Burke's diagnosis was different. He sensed, quite correctly, that the media would run with the story as a "Johnson & Johnson problem," that the government would view it as a public health problem, and that the company's customers would define the problem as simply fear of Johnson & Johnson's products.

A talent for understanding what facts and events mean to others is especially valuable when managers confront difficult ethical issues.

These issues often stimulate intense feelings and conflicts, and disagreements about values can be interpreted as attacks on others'
character and integrity. And the managers who must resolve difficult
ethical issues are just as vulnerable to these hazards as anyone else.
For example, when Adario devised his plan, he was convinced he
was, unambiguously, doing the right thing: McNeil would keep her
job and the IBM account would get back on schedule. Having
positioned himself firmly on the moral high ground, Adario thought
Walters and the vice president were the ones in need of ethical
guidance.

Adario might have fared better had he worked hard to answer a
second basic question for managers whose organizations face defining moments: What is the cash value of this situation and of my
ideas for the people whose support I need? A sound answer to this
question might have helped Adario refine his message and shape it
to the specific psychological and political context in which he was
working.

TRUTH *HAPPENS* TO AN IDEA

William James had another valuable insight about truth, one that
expresses something that leaders like James Burke understand and
that managers like Peter Adario need to learn. Like his idea that
"truth works," it seems to depart from the standard correspondence
(or dead-bug) view of truth. James's insight was this: "The truth of
an idea is not a stagnant property inherent in it. Truth *happens* to
an idea. It *becomes* true, is *made* true by events. Its verity *is* in fact an
event, a process."[10]

This is a profoundly important way for managers to think about
defining moments. Viewed from this perspective, a defining moment
for an organization is far more than a courageous executive decision
or a climactic event like Johnson & Johnson's decision to recall all
Tylenol capsules. The final, dramatic moment is often only the final
and most visible part of a complex political, psychological, and
administrative process. To think otherwise is to mistake an exclama-
tion point for the sentence that precedes it.

For managers, process does the heavy lifting. It gives victory to one interpretation, defines it as "the truth" for an organization, and makes a defining moment possible. What Adario had forgotten about the Tylenol episode was all that preceded it. He was impressed by what the company did; he should have been impressed that it was *ready* to do what it did.

Burke's actions, in the moment of crisis, were only the latest in a long series of efforts to renew the company's commitment to its basic values. The company credo was decades old and closely associated with the company's revered, long-time chairman, General Robert Johnson, who created it. The credo had been carefully crafted, occasionally updated and clarified, and, above all, it had proven to be good business. By ranking mothers and doctors well ahead of shareholders in its priorities, it discouraged short-sighted profit seek- ing that risked the entire firm's reputation. Moreover, several years before the Tylenol episode, Burke had asked the company's execu- tives whether the credo was still relevant, and the ensuing discussions reaffirmed its value to the company. Even the Zomax episode and the negative publicity resulting from it may have encouraged Johnson & Johnson to take its credo more seriously.

Because truth is a process, Adario's campaign for a more family- friendly workplace should have begun *even before* McNeil began work- ing at Sayer MicroWorld. From the start, Adario should have realized the difficult, vulnerable position he was putting McNeil in. For example, McNeil had told him during a recruiting interview that she had firm plans for child care and would be able to work ten- hour days. That statement alone, unfortunately, was good enough for Adario. He gave no thought to several other equally plausible scenarios. Her day-care arrangements might fall through, as these arrangements often do. Her son would occasionally be sick, and she would need to stay with him or take him to the doctor. And the wear and tear of single parenthood and a demanding job would eventually take their toll on McNeil. Even if he had asked about these contingencies, and even if McNeil had said she was prepared for them, Adario should have been skeptical and planned accord- ingly, especially because almost everyone trims his or her sails to raise the chances of a job offer.

Adario also erred when he told McNeil that there would be only rare occasions when she had to work at night or on weekends. This was careless, if not naive. Adario knew that the company's position was too fragile and its industry too turbulent to project a schedule like this into the future.

Worse, neither McNeil nor Adario asked the hard questions about how family-friendly Sayer MicroWorld really was. Its executives gave lip service to the idea but had no policies in place. Whereas most people endorse "family-friendly" policies in theory, especially when the rhetoric from headquarters makes it the politically correct thing to do, their views can change when the pressure builds and they have to pick up the slack for a parent who is falling behind schedule. More candor and realism, even a dose of skepticism, might have helped both Adario and McNeil understand the challenges that she might face at Sayer MicroWorld.

After he decided to hire McNeil, Adario should have taken other steps to lay the groundwork for her success. It was crucial, for example, for Adario's superiors, as well as her coworkers, to support his decision to hire her. In particular, he needed to help them understand the skills and experience, particularly with IBM, that she brought to the company. He also could have created opportunities for them to get to know her personally, or even to meet her son, in order to help others understand and appreciate what she was accomplishing.

Once McNeil started work, Adario could have supported her in other ways. For example, he could have let his bosses know how hard she was working and all that she was accomplishing. This might have given her some allies at headquarters, making it more difficult for Walters to go over Adario's head and get her fired so quickly.

In short, Adario didn't realize that a defining moment is only one step in a long and complex process. Unfortunately, he did almost no spadework. Then, when a crisis occurred, he defined the issue as a scheduling problem or an interpersonal misunderstanding and hoped that one successful meeting would induce everyone to rise with him and salute the "family-friendly" flag. Adario had failed to think through the third basic question about defining moments for organizations: Have I orchestrated a process that can make the values I care about become the truth for my organization?

PLAYING FOR KEEPS

Machiavelli would probably have listened politely to most of the advice given to Peter Adario in this chapter. The idea that truth is an interpretation that works, that powerful ideas have cash value, and that truth is a process—all these ideas are consistent with his view of the world. But Machiavelli would have had more advice for Adario.

In all likelihood, he would have viewed Adario's world of mergers, debt, layoffs, and bureaucratic maneuvering as child's play, in contrast to the perils and treachery of Renaissance Italy. There people's lives—including Machiavelli's, at one point—sometimes hung in the balance. Machiavelli was, above all, a lifelong student of what Peter Drucker has called managing in turbulent times.

Adario might have been shocked at Machiavelli's first question: How much longer did Adario expect to keep his job? Lisa Walters's star was clearly on the rise. While Adario was out of the office, she worked with one of his bosses to swiftly resolve an important issue he had neglected. The vice president didn't reprimand her for going over Adario's head; no one even suggested she go through the formalities of consulting him. On this decision, Adario was a non-person.

Contests of interpretation, Machiavelli would tell Adario, can be power struggles. The victorious interpretation can determine not just the values of a company, but bonuses, promotions, and careers. If Walters didn't have her eye on his job before McNeil was fired, she probably did afterward, because top management seemed to like her take-charge style. While Adario was lobbing nice, underhand softball pitches, Walters was playing hardball. Machiavelli's question to managers facing defining moments for their organizations is this: Are you playing to win?

He might also mention that winning is more than having the biggest pile of goodies—money, perks, titles, and so forth—at the end of the game. Nietzsche believed that deeper, more powerful forces—which he called the "will to power"—fueled people's motives and shaped their interpretations of events. He wrote, "We seek a picture of the world in that philosophy in which we feel freest; that is, in which our most powerful drive feels free to function."[11] In other words, Walters's disagreement with Adario may well express bedrock personal assumptions about life, work, and ethics. When the stakes are this high, people play the games of organizational life to win.

In a world like this, the simple, inspiring, do-the-right-thing view of ethics is a path to obscure martyrdom. Machiavelli condemned leaders who sought to live in "imaginary worlds" of ethical aspirations, while failing to take action in this world. Adario had failed to help McNeil, perhaps placed his own job at risk, and threatened the security of his family. Adario's heart was in the right place when he hired McNeil. He believed she could do the job, he admired her courage, and he wanted to lend her a helping hand and create a workplace in which she could prosper. All this was genuinely commendable. But such praiseworthy intentions need support and protection, in the form of a talent for maneuvering, shrewdness, and political savvy.

James Burke had honed these skills to a very high level, and he used them brilliantly during the two Tylenol episodes. A remarkable example occurred in 1986, after another poisoning death led Johnson & Johnson to announce that it would no longer sell capsule products over the counter. Burke had agreed to a live television interview, and an enterprising reporter, with an instinct for the jugular, said this to him: "The mother of Diane Ellsroth, the girl who was killed, said she feels that Johnson & Johnson was three years too late. What is your response to that?"

The reporter was trying to ask a question that might catch Burke off guard. She was appealing directly and dramatically to the sympathy of the audience. She was suggesting, rather unsubtly, that Burke and his company had contributed to the death of an innocent young woman.

Burke had no time to prepare an answer. He was facing a camera under the hot lights of a television studio. The stakes were very high: Johnson & Johnson had spent vast sums to rebuild its image and Tylenol's market share after the 1982 calamity. Burke was addressing a world in which admitting a mistake invites lawsuits, in which defensiveness or evasion by an executive triggers cynicism, and in which a company reputation, like a piece of crystal created over months, can be destroyed in a moment. Here is Burke's answer:

> *My response is that if I were the mother of Diane Ellsroth, I'd say the same thing. And I'd feel the same thing. And with the benefit of hindsight, which is 20-20, I wish we'd never gone back into the market with capsules myself.*[12]

This three-sentence answer, spoken in less than ten seconds, is remarkable—for what Burke did and did not say. He managed to walk right through the reporter's trap, with his reputation and Johnson & Johnson's intact. Burke did not change the subject. He did not say, "We did the best we could," or that the real villain was whoever poisoned the capsule, or that Johnson & Johnson was also a victim. He responded directly to the reporter's question, without hesitation or diversion.

Like the reporter, Burke also appealed to the audience's feelings, saying he would feel and say just what the mother had said. This made it clear he was a human being who understood the tragedy of this mother and daughter. At the same time, while he expressed regrets about the original capsule decision, he briefly mentioned that 20-20 hindsight lay behind his view. This enabled him to express regret without making a statement that could be used against his company in court.

Peter Adario showed few of the skills that Burke had plainly mastered. He missed subtle signals and patterns—which would have indicated to him that another process, quite opposed to his intentions, was already under way. Recall that Lisa Walters had sent Adario two notes, each suggesting that McNeil be replaced. What were these notes really about? Were they trial balloons, proposals, tentative announcements of a plan, or tests of Adario's authority, since he was supposed to make decisions like this? And what did Walters make of the fact that Adario didn't respond to her first note? Did this mean he was too busy, that the issue wasn't important enough, that he thought Walters was on the right track, that he was vacillating and she could take the initiative, that he didn't think her concerns were that important? Walters apparently interpreted his reaction as indicating that he wouldn't stand in the way of firing McNeil. Walters may have even thought that Adario wanted McNeil fired but was unwilling to do it himself.

Moreover, Adario should have realized much earlier that Walters was a threat to McNeil and to the values he wanted to instill in his department. Recall that she was reluctant to hire McNeil in the first place and that she and others in the department were inclined to bulldoze their decisions through the organization. None of this, by itself, may have meant much. Together, however, they formed a pattern that should have put Adario on alert.

Machiavelli would have admired Adario if, from the beginning, even before McNeil was hired, Adario had taken steps to get Walters on board or at least keep her from making mischief. Instead, Machiavelli probably would have commended Lisa Walters, at least for her short-term tactics. She didn't overreach, timed her moves carefully, and had found herself a powerful ally, the vice president who helped her carry out her plan.

Adario would have fared better if he had thought carefully about four important questions: What are the other strong, persuasive, competing interpretations of the situation or problem that I hope to use as a defining moment for my organization? What is the cash value of this situation and of my ideas for the people whose support I need? Have I orchestrated a process that can make the values I care about become the truth for my organization? Am I playing to win?

TRAINING IN LOSING

Machiavelli might have pressed Adario to answer a last question, one in which the political becomes the personal. How much did Adario really care about creating a family-friendly department and helping Kathryn McNeil? Adario's efforts had run counter to one of Machiavelli's bedrock convictions:

> *He will be successful who directs his actions to the spirit of the times. . . . One can see of two cautious men the one attain his end, the other fail; and similarly, two men by different observances are equally successful, the*

one being cautious, the other impetuous; all this arises from nothing else than whether or not they conform in their methods to the spirit of the times.[13]

Adario should have realized from the beginning that he was battling "the spirit of the times" in his company. Did he want to continue doing so now? If Adario wanted to view himself as an organization man, or as a good butler like Stevens, his path would now be clear. McNeil's job was lost, the organization's values were defined, and now he needed to protect his own job. But the damage-control tactics Machiavelli might recommend would completely overlook the fact that Adario's failure could also be a personal defining moment, like Steve Lewis's decision about the St. Louis presentation.

Like Lewis, Adario now had to decide whether there were some lines he would not cross. Should he fight McNeil's firing? Should he make clear that he disagreed with it? Should he say he supported the decision but with reservations. Or should he say that Walters had done what he was planning to do? When Adario chooses among these alternatives, as he must, he will be revealing and testing some of his basic values and also, as Nietzsche would emphasize, choosing his future self. Nietzsche would likely view Adario's choice in similar terms. Adario now needs to answer Nietzsche's challenge, "This is my way; where is yours?"

Peter Adario might think otherwise and view this as a young person's issue. After all, Adario had already worked for 14 years at three different firms; he was married, had children, and knew a lot about the computer industry. His major commitments in life seemed to be behind him. He thought he knew who he was and what he stood for, and his successful career suggested he had made the right choices. But this way of thinking would repel Nietzsche. He condemned complacency about oneself, writing that "All those who are in the process of becoming must be furious when they perceive some satisfaction in this area, an impertinent 'retiring on one's laurels' or 'self-congratulation.' "[14] One of his foremost interpreters observed that, for Nietzsche, "The creation of the self is not a static episode, a final goal which, once attained, forecloses the possibility of continuing to change and develop."[15]

From Nietzsche's perspective, then, Adario's failure was actually an opportunity for learning and personal growth. After Roger Hansen's suicide, an acquaintance commented that "People who breeze through high school and college the way Denny did get no training in losing." No one enjoys losing, and some people never recover from failures. Nevertheless, Nietzsche's rather romantic declaration that "What does not kill me makes me stronger" contains an important element of truth for managers.

For Adario, who had long worked and lived in the flow of success, the experience of adversity proved valuable. He told his boss, the vice president, that he disagreed with the decision to fire Kathryn McNeil and objected strongly to the way the decision was made. He then told Lisa Walters that her behavior would be reflected in the next performance review he put in her file. Neither Walters nor the vice president said much in response, and for months afterward Adario lived and worked in a state of limbo. He feared he had imperiled his job, but the issue never arose again.

What had Adario learned? He found he had much more ambivalence about his job. He was grateful to have it, despite its demands, mainly because he believed he had come close to losing it. At the same time, he was more aware of the arbitrariness and potential harshness of the business system in which he worked. After all, he had watched Kathryn McNeil, a devoted mother and a hard and talented worker, lose her job on four hours' notice and walk out the door, in tears, with two weeks of severance pay. He later learned that she was unemployed for five months after she was fired.

Adario also felt he had rid himself of a naive view of what it takes to redefine the values of an organization, even a small one like his department. He now viewed the Johnson & Johnson story—both the Tylenol and the Zomax episodes—in a new light. He realized that he needed to get his hands dirty, in Sartre's sense of the term. This meant thinking and acting more shrewdly and realistically, so that he and the people who relied on him would not, once again, climb out on a limb and ignore the sawing noises behind them. Adario now understood that managers could meet their ethical responsibilities only if they had excellent managerial and political skills, and he felt he had begun to understand this in a instinctive way, as a result of his frustrating and painful experience.

Finally, Adario found himself reexamining how the pieces of his life were fitting together. His failure led not to a midlife crisis, but to something nearer to a midlife reconsideration.[16] The relentless pace of his work had strained his marriage, left his children near the bottom of his to-do list, and made him an accomplice in firing a hard-working, admirable employee. Was this the path he wanted? In Aristotle's terms, were these the practices and habits that he wanted to shape his character? From James's perspective, did it offer "vital satisfactions," and was it "good for life"?

Clearly, the question "This is my way; where is yours?" is not merely relevant to Adario, but crucial. And, by reflecting on the issues it raises, Adario would raise his odds of avoiding the fate of another middle-aged middle manager, the butler Stevens.

8

↔

Virtu, *Virtue, and Success*

T HE RU 486 DECISION represents the most complex
type of defining moment. Edouard Sakiz, the chairman of
Roussel-Uclaf, had to choose among many compelling responsibilities: to his conscience, shareholders, employees, women,
physicians, scientists, government health agencies, and—in the
minds of his vigilant, well-organized critics—to the unborn. All
these right-versus-right tradeoffs converged on Sakiz's desk.

At the same time, the RU 486 decision was a defining moment for
Sakiz personally. He had responsibilities as a physician, a scientist, a
manager, a shareholder's agent, a citizen, and a family member.
Like Steve Lewis and Peter Adario, Sakiz's actions would indicate
which of these responsibilities had the deepest roots in his life.
The decision would likely be Sakiz's legacy as an executive, as a
medical researcher, and perhaps as a human being. In Nietzsche's
terms, it would define "his way."

The RU 486 decision would also be a defining moment for
Roussel-Uclaf. Within the company, there was passionate disagreement on what its commitment to "the service of Life" meant in this
case. Some believed the company was morally obligated to

introduce the drug; some employees were circulating letters encouraging others to become "conscientious objectors" to the drug; others feared the political vortex into which the company was being drawn. Even the executive committee was split: two members favored introducing RU 486 and two opposed it. Everyone was watching Sakiz intently. His actions would be decisive, for RU 486 and for the company.

The contest of interpretations within Roussel-Uclaf parallels Peter Adario's battle with Lisa Walters, albeit on a much larger and more complex scale, because Sakiz was also engaged in a high-stakes power struggle involving his boss and his subordinates. While the management board of Hoechst, the 55 percent owner of Roussel-Uclaf, was split on RU 486, its chairman was a Roman Catholic who opposed abortion in general and RU 486 in particular. At the same time, two of the executives who reported to Sakiz also opposed introducing the drug. Sakiz, like Peter Adario, could get caught in the middle.

Sakiz's decision on RU 486 would be a defining moment in a third important sense. It would be a critical juncture in the long process that would define his company's role in society and its relationships with its many stakeholders. Government bodies, the media, and interest groups would all react to whatever the company did. Their reactions would in turn influence the company's ability to carry out its decisions—on RU 486 and, in years to come, on other products. Some of Roussel-Uclaf's stakeholders were friendly, others were hostile. Each had its own agenda. Hence, Sakiz could not unilaterally define his company's role in society. It would emerge over time from the company's dealings—cooperative as well as adversarial—with many other parties.

Sakiz's decision was extraordinarily complex. He would be revealing, testing, and in some ways shaping his own ethics. Like Steve Lewis, Sakiz had to make a defining personal choice, one that would form an important part of his life and his career. At the same time, his decision would define some of the basic values of his organization, as well as its relationships with its stakeholders.

"SUSPENDING DISTRIBUTION"

In late October 1988, a month after the French government approved RU 486, Sakiz and the executive committee of Roussel-Uclaf made their decision. The *New York Times* described the decision in these words:

> *At an October 21 meeting, Sakiz surprised members of the management committee by calling for a discussion of RU 486. There, in Roussel-Uclaf's ultra-modern board room, the pill's longstanding opponents repeated their objections: RU 486 could spark a painful boycott, it was hurting employee morale, management was devoting too much of its energy to defending itself in this controversy. Finally, it would never be hugely profitable, because much would be sold on cost basis to the Third World.*
>
> *After two hours, Sakiz again stunned the committee by calling for a vote. When he raised his own hand in favor of suspending distribution of RU 486, it was clear that the pill was doomed.*[1]

In an interview after the vote, Sakiz said, "We have a responsibility in managing a company. But if I were a lone scientist, I would have acted differently."[2]

The company informed its employees of the decision on October 25. The next day, Roussel-Uclaf announced publicly that "it was suspending distribution of the drug because of pressure from anti-abortion groups." A Roussel-Uclaf official explained, "The pressure groups in the United States are very powerful, maybe even more so than in France. We see that in the American presidential campaign abortion is a major subject of debate, but in France people speak less and less of it."[3]

The company's decision, and Sakiz's role in it, sparked astonishment and anger. The company and its leadership, critics charged, had doomed a promising public health tool and set an example of cowardice. For example, a colleague and friend of Sakiz's, Dr. Etienne-Emile Baulieu, whose research had been crucial to developing RU 486, called the decision "morally scandalous" and accused Sakiz of caving in to pressure. Other critics suggested sarcastically that the company's decision was no surprise, because Roussel-Uclaf had decided, in the face of controversy during the 1960s, not to produce contraceptive pills.

Three days after Roussel-Uclaf announced that it would suspend distribution, the French minister of health summoned Roussel-Uclaf's vice chairman to his office and said that, if the company did not resume distribution, the government would transfer the patent to a company that would. (Under French intellectual property law, the government could take a patent from one company and give it to another if this served the national interest.) After the meeting with the minister of health, Roussel-Uclaf announced that it would distribute RU 486 after all.

These events suggest that the RU 486 episode was something considerably less than a profile in courage. In his defining moment, Edouard Sakiz seems to have protected his job by sacrificing his convictions. There was, to be sure, strong opposition to RU 486, both inside and outside his company, but Sakiz made no effort to mobilize and lead his allies. He gave up without a fight. As a defining moment for the company, Sakiz's message seemed to place political caution and returns to shareholders above research and "the service of Life."

WHAT IS SUCCESS?

Machiavelli would have shaken his head in dismay at these criticisms. They would have sounded superficial, sentimental, and naive to him. Of the critics who called Sakiz a failure, he would have asked, "Just what is success?" Machiavelli had a clear answer to this question, one that would have led him to judge Sakiz in a different light.

Machiavelli celebrated secure, far-sighted rulers who presided over prosperous, stable, peaceful states. They provided his image and ideal of success. One of Machiavelli's foremost contemporary observers, Sir Isaiah Berlin, wrote that

> *Like the Roman writers whose ideals were constantly before his mind, like Cicero and Livy, Machiavelli believed that what men—at any rate superior men—sought was the fulfillment and the glory that come from the creation*

and maintenance by common endeavor of a strong and well-governed social whole.[4]

But how does a leader accomplish this? Machiavelli's answer is fascinating and acutely relevant to turbulent times. It is also complex and therefore easily misinterpreted. Elizabethan dramatists, for example, selected Machiavelli's most alarming precepts to create the image of the "murd'rous Machiavel." Many others have followed their example. But the simple, one-sided Machiavelli would not have intrigued so many powerful minds for more than four centuries. Worse, the standard stereotype ignores important aspects of Machiavelli's writings. He did not condemn morality or Christianity. In fact, he writes explicitly that deception, betrayal, and murder are no cause for glory, and the princes he admired were hardly narrow, self-interested figures grasping at power.

Machiavelli's central insight was that successful leaders have to follow a special ethical code, one that differs from their private morality and from Judeo-Christian ethics. "Public life," in Isaiah Berlin's words, "has its own morality."[5] He explains Machiavelli's view with an analogy:

To be a physician is to be a professional, ready to burn, to cauterise, to amputate; if that is what the disease requires, then to stop half-way because of personal qualms, or some rule unrelated to your art and its technique, is a sign of muddle and weakness, and will always give you the worst of both worlds. . . . There is more than one world, and more than one set of virtues: confusion between them is disastrous.[6]

Virtu was Machiavelli's word for the moral code of public life. The word is not an antiquated version of *virtue*, for it means something quite different. *Virtu* is a combination of vigor, confidence, imagination, shrewdness, boldness, practical skill, personal force, determination, and self-discipline. Machiavelli acknowledges without hesitation that *virtu* would be irrelevant if everyone were virtuous and cooperative, but that was not his experience. One authority on Machiavelli's era writes, "Cities were torn by feud and vendetta. . . .

Alliances were forged only to be broken, the countryside was constantly scarred by pillage, rapine, and battle, and in this maelstrom the old bonds of society were broken and new ones forged."[7]

Sakiz's world, and that of many other senior executives, closely parallels Machiavelli's. The counterpart of "feud and vendetta" is the ceaseless internal politics of most companies, especially in an era when no job is secure and senior executives are rewarded with spectacularly high incomes. The counterpart of the external dangers and shifting alliances that Machiavelli studied are hostile takeovers and the typically unstable strategic alliances that companies forge with competitors, as well as with suppliers and customers who can become tomorrow's competitors. The government agencies, labor unions, interest groups, local communities, and media are all potential allies and adversaries. Some stakeholders form valuable partnerships with companies; others fight companies with force and tenacity. Market competition is relentless and unforgiving, as is the media in many cases.

Under these circumstances, the creation of a growing, stable, profitable business is a remarkable accomplishment. Introducing a pioneering product—especially one like RU 486, which, in Machiavelli's phrase, "changes the order of things"—is exceedingly complex and hazardous. *Virtu*, Machiavelli would say, is indispensable in such a situation; only a naive manager would think otherwise.

MACHIAVELLI'S QUESTIONS

Three questions can help managers translate *virtu* into practical terms. These questions summarize the guidance Machiavelli would give managers who must define their companies' role in society and their relationships with important stakeholders. The questions also provide standards—Machiavelli's standards, to be sure—for assessing Edouard Sakiz's actions.

The first question follows directly from Machiavelli's view that weak leaders and fragile organizations accomplish little in this world, for good or ill, because they are preoccupied with survival. Hence the first question: Have I done all I can to secure my position and the strength and stability of my organization? Machiavelli also firmly believed that fortune favors the bold, so the second question is: Have I thought creatively and imaginatively about my organization's role in society and its relationship to its stakeholders? The third question expresses Machiavelli's concern with selecting the right tactics for particular situations. In Chapter 18 of *The Prince*, Machiavelli writes that successful leaders must be capable of acting like either lions or foxes, depending on the circumstances. His explanation is that "the lion cannot defend himself against snares and the fox cannot defend himself against wolves."[8] Hence the third question: Should I play the lion or the fox?

To assess what Sakiz did, we must examine his actions in light of these three questions, beginning with the third. Only a careful examination of Sakiz's tactics will indicate whether he was indeed seeking a secure foundation for Roussel-Uclaf and whether he had defined its role in society creatively.

Clearly, Sakiz was no lion. He waved no flags and charged no hills. Unlike James Burke, he is no one's candidate for canonization. Machiavelli, however, had misgivings about lions. He knew there are times when leaders had to rely on the fearless, decisive stroke, and he understood the popular appeal of heroes and saints. Nevertheless, Machiavelli believed that foxes were better equipped to survive and prosper. "Those who rely simply on the lion do not know what they are about," he wrote. "He who has known best how to employ the fox has succeeded best."[9]

Foxes are stealthy, wary, sharp, and quick. They are masters of nuance, maneuver, and subtlety. Foxes are comfortable with circuitous paths. They wait patiently, watch astutely, and then dart at opportunity. Before judging Sakiz, Machiavelli would want to know whether he had decided to "employ the fox." The answer lies in examining the nuances of what Sakiz did and did not do, the process he set in motion, and the results the company achieved.

Consider, first, what Roussel-Uclaf did *not* do. It did not say that RU 486 was unethical or that distribution of the product would violate the company credo. Roussel-Uclaf did not say it was abandoning its plans to market RU 486, only that it would "suspend distribution." There was no indication of how long the suspension would last. And Sakiz did not even say that he stood firmly behind the decision; instead, he revealed that he would have made a different decision if he had been "a lone scientist."

Consider some of the other fine details of the company's announcement. It said that "pressure from anti-abortion groups" was responsible for its decision. This was an invitation for abortion rights groups to mobilize. The company had announced, in effect, that its decision depended on the vector sum of external pressures. Presumably, enough pressure from the other side could end the suspension of distribution. The company also emphasized the pressures from outside France, particularly the United States. Here was another implicit invitation: to defend the autonomy of a French company (and, implicitly, the independence and dignity of the French nation?) against American pressure groups and powerful German business executives.

The process Sakiz relied on is also telling. Once again, nuance is crucial. Recall that the timing of the vote on RU 486 was a surprise, even to the management committee. Yet it coincided exactly with the meeting of the World Congress of Gynecology and Obstetrics in Rio de Janeiro. A strong majority of its members supported RU 486. Roussel-Uclaf's decision to suspend distribution spurred the group to action. Led by Baulieu, who said he was acting with Sakiz's encouragement, the physicians made RU 486 the focus of their meeting. Ultimately, hundreds of doctors signed a petition condemning Roussel-Uclaf and threatening to boycott both Roussel-Uclaf and Hoechst.

This reaction was amplified by the intense media coverage of Roussel-Uclaf's decision. Sakiz had provided journalists with a man-bites-dog story. No one expected Sakiz, who participated in the early research leading to RU 486 and then sponsored its development, to repudiate his years of effort and commitment. Moreover, Roussel-Uclaf had invested many years and millions of dollars developing RU 486 and had recently applied for permission to introduce it. No one expected the company to veer from its path. As a result, there was widespread astonishment when Sakiz voted with the drug's opponents.

Because Sakiz shattered expectations, he seized the attention of the media and of abortion rights groups around the world. A front-page headline in the *New York Times* read "Drug Maker Stops All Distribution of Abortion Pill; Pressure of Foes Cited." News stories like this triggered an explosion of criticism of Roussel-Uclaf from women's groups, family planning advocates, and physicians in the United States and Europe. The reaction at the medical conference in Brazil led to another front-page headline: "Doctors Protest Company's Action on Abortion Pill; Withdrawal Denounced."

The surprising reversal of Roussel-Uclaf's original decision prompted relief among abortion rights groups, dismay among abortion opponents, and suspicion among many observers. Some wondered if the company and the government had choreographed the entire episode. Others noted that government science and health officials and Roussel-Uclaf managers and researchers had worked together for years—on RU 486, on other products, and on many other regulatory issues. Moreover, the French government was one of the company's major shareholders. Given this close, long-term relationship, explicit planning may have been unnecessary. Parties who know each other well can coordinate their efforts with little more than a wink and a nod, following what the French sometimes call the "rule of anticipated reactions." In short, they can act like foxes.

Sakiz seemed to have paid close attention to a series of questions that Machiavelli believed to be critical: What allies do I have, inside and outside my company? What allies do I need? Which parties will resist or fight my efforts? Have I underestimated their power and tactical skill or overestimated their ethics? Can I respond quickly and flexibly, thereby seizing opportunities?

Sakiz apparently had little interest in being a solitary, glorious, dead lion. He chose, instead, to maneuver behind the scenes, test the strength and commitment of his potential allies, and then let the strongest of them, the French government, take responsibility for the final decision on RU 486.

ONE JUDGES BY THE RESULT

Interpretations like these are, of course, somewhat speculative—neither Roussel-Uclaf nor Sakiz gives interviews on the subject. But the view that Sakiz "employed the fox" can be tested by examining the results of the events that were triggered by Sakiz's vote against RU 486. This is exactly how Machiavelli would analyze a situation in which the protagonists have no incentive to reveal their true intentions. Everyone, Machiavelli writes, knows what a prince appears to be, but few know what a prince really is or what a leader really thinks. For cases like these, he gives this advice: "in the actions of all men, and especially of princes, which it is not prudent to challenge, one judges by the result."[10]

What had Sakiz accomplished? More specifically, had he protected and advanced his own position? Had he contributed to the strength and security of his company? And had he defined its role in society in a creative way?

In personal terms, Sakiz succeeded in making good on his personal commitment to RU 486—Roussel-Uclaf would distribute the drug, first in France and later elsewhere. At the same time, he protected his job against the chairman of Hoechst. Because the French government had ordered Roussel-Uclaf to distribute the drug, Hoechst would accomplish little by replacing Sakiz with an opponent of RU 486. In fact, such an action would likely aggravate the French health ministry, which could retaliate against Hoechst in various ways, since it regulated the Roussel-Uclaf and Hoechst products sold in France.

For Roussel-Uclaf employees, the period of uncertainty and speculation was over, and the company decision was clear. Roussel-Uclaf would sell RU 486 with the support of the French government. Any opposition to the decision or to Sakiz was now futile. But the final decision was not Sakiz's alone—it was the French government's—so some hard feelings, though surely not all, would be diverted from Sakiz to the ministry. After all, the government was now ultimately responsible for putting RU 486 on the market. The minister of health had taken unambiguous responsibility when he said, "I could not permit the abortion debate to deprive women of a product that represents medical progress." Sakiz could hope that subsequent anti-abortion protests would be directed against the French government, rather than against Roussel-Uclaf, Hoechst, and their shareholders. The company even suggested as much—once again, subtley—when the company's vice chairman commented, just after meeting with the minister of health, "We are relieved of the moral burden weighing on our shoulders." In other words, the moral burden rested elsewhere, so protesters and boycotters should paint their bull's-eyes on other organizational targets.

Finally, how had Sakiz defined Roussel-Uclaf's role in society? He certainly did not take the easy way out. Sakiz could have pleased his boss in Germany and avoided years of controversy and boycotts by withdrawing entirely from the market for contraceptives and other reproductive drugs, which is what virtually all American drug companies have done. To justify this approach, he could have defined Roussel-Uclaf's social role in standard, familiar terms, as the property of its shareholders. Thus, he could have argued, RU 486 had to be shelved, because boycotts against Roussel-Uclaf and Hoechst were likely to cost far more than the drug would earn.

Instead, Sakiz seems to have defined Roussel-Uclaf's role in a remarkable, perhaps even daring way. It would be a political activist and catalyst. The company worked to stimulate and then shape media coverage; it invited its allies to mobilize after dismaying them by suspending distribution; it acceded to government intervention that it may have encouraged or even arranged; and it tried to blur responsibility for the introduction of RU 486.

Roussel-Uclaf was committed to "the service of Life"—following an original, complex, and daring strategy. Women seeking nonsurgical abortions and their physicians would be among the company's core stakeholders. Hence, Roussel-Uclaf would distribute RU 486, first in France and then elsewhere, but neither Sakiz nor his company had volunteered for martyrdom.

ARISTOTLE'S QUESTION

Here are Machiavelli's lessons for managers whose decisions will define their company's role in society and its relations with stakeholders. First, don't be confused about success. Success means having a strong and prosperous organization, for the weak and impecunious can do little good. Second, watch your adversaries; don't overestimate their ethics or underestimate their power. Third, remember that managers cannot simply define their company's role in society;

they must negotiate it. Therefore, be fluid and seize opportunity—sometimes play the lion; more often, the fox. And, in all cases, rely on *virtu*. These are important lessons. Steve Lewis tempered his virtuous aspirations with shrewd practicality and scored a minor personal and professional triumph. Peter Adario exemplified virtue without *virtu* and got nowhere.

But Machiavelli's lessons are also disconcerting; many famous and powerful scoundrels practice *virtu* without virtue and make the world a worse place. Clearly, there is an urgent need to find other lessons for managers who face choices like Sakiz's. The writings of Aristotle, who developed the foremost theory of human virtue, are an excellent place to find such lessons. At the heart of Aristotle's thinking about sound moral decisions is an idea commonly called "the golden mean." Unfortunately, this phrase, coined ages ago by the Roman poet Horace, has become so familiar that it conceals and almost trivializes an extraordinarily powerful and useful idea.

For Aristotle, the principle of the golden mean is the master key to virtue. Here is how he describes the principle, in one of the most famous and influential passages in all of moral philosophy:

> it is in the nature of moral qualities that they are destroyed by deficiency and excess, just as we can see . . . in the case of health and strength. For both excessive and insufficient exercise destroy one's strength, and both eating and drinking too much or too little destroy health, whereas the right quantity produces, increases and preserves it. So it is the same with temperance, courage and the other virtues. The man who shuns and fears everything and stands up to nothing becomes a coward; the man who is afraid of nothing at all, but marches up to every danger, becomes foolhardy.[11]

At first glance, Aristotle's view is a bit disappointing. High ideals, undying faith, and passionate commitment all seem to have vanished from the sphere of ethics. In their place, Aristotle advocates moderation, circumspection, restraint. He offers an ethics of measured reactions, calibrated moves, and judicious compromise. All this may be practical, but it is also as dry as dust.

Why does Aristotle seem to endorse an ethics of accountants over one of heroes and saints? His answer is simple. He believed that excess or deficiency could literally "destroy" moral qualities. Excess turns good into evil, virtue into vice. Men and women, he believed, should avoid moral commitments that risk or ruin lives. Antigone and Creon, for example, both faced the same ethical issue: finding the appropriate way to treat the body of Antigone's brother, who had died a rebel in a bloody civil war. The question pitted piety and family loyalty against an urgent need to restore civil order and avoid more bloodshed. Both Antigone and Creon answered the question with passionate commitment to opposing ethical ideals. Neither left an inch for compromise, so they condemned themselves and their families to an awful fate.

Were Aristotle alive today, at the close of our bloody century, he would find an abundance of tragic evidence to support his deliberate, judicious style of ethics. Countless episodes of cruelty, terrorism, and mass slaughter have been perpetrated by leaders who could not compromise their exacting political principles. Other killers have been inflamed by religious ideals, translating the Bible, Koran, or other sacred texts into merciless bloodshed.

Aristotle counsels moderation and caution precisely because he is giving advice for situations in which important ethical claims stand in opposition. He wants to discourage men and women who find tension or conflict among their duties, commitments, responsibilities, and virtues from veering too sharply in one direction or another and trampling on some fundamental human values as they pursue others. This is why Stuart Hampshire has written that, for Aristotle, "balance represents a deep moral ideal in a world of inescapable conflicts."[12]

The ideal of balance provides valuable guidance for managers who must resolve right-versus-right conflicts—especially those, like Edouard Sakiz's, that pit so many important values and responsibilities against each other. Aristotle's question for managers would be this: Have you done all you can to strike a balance, both morally and practically? By Aristotle's standard of balance, Sakiz performed quite well. His effort illustrates four aspects of balance that matter greatly when managers must define their firms' role in society and relations to their stakeholders.

First, balance is a standard for assessing the ends or aims a manager pursues. Aristotle's ideal of balance implicitly asks someone in Sakiz's position—or Lewis's or Adario's—to make sure that their dilemma does indeed pit one ethical responsibility against another. The golden mean isn't a device for calibrating the right amount to steal, the right number of workers to exploit, or—to borrow Aristotle's example—the right way to commit adultery.

In other words, the deceptive maneuvering we have attributed to Sakiz would not have been ethically justified if his aim were to raise his year-end bonus and buy a nice condominium. *Virtu*, Aristotle would argue, must serve ethical ends. So, too, must actions that create dirty hands. Only ethical ends can vindicate unethical means. The defense of Sakiz's maneuvers thus rests on the fact that he was pursuing ethical aims and commitments. Moreover, his tactics seemed the most practical and the least dishonest path he could find though the labyrinth of his moral responsibilities.

Balance is also a standard, for assessing means or tactics. Sakiz also fares well by this standard because his steps were moderate and cautious. He carefully avoided extremes and points of no return. Sakiz was clear about his personal support for RU 486, but he didn't try to lead a public crusade on its behalf. Doing so might have escalated the boycott and raised costs to shareholders; it also might have cost him his job, and with it the opportunity to pursue the ethical aims to which RU 486 was essential. At the same time, Sakiz did not put on his shareholder's agent hat, run the numbers, and return RU 486 to the laboratory shelf because of its financial risks. Veering too sharply in the direction of his boss's and shareholders' concerns would have violated other important ideals. In short, Sakiz chose tactics that let him follow a middle path.

He was also moderate in his departure from the full truth. Faced with the prospect of dirty hands, he kept his hands as clean as possible. Sakiz did not conceal his support for RU 486, the suspension did turn out to be temporary, and the reasons he gave for the suspension—the antiabortion campaign, especially in the United States—were accurate, if incomplete. What Sakiz did not do was disclose his entire plan, nor did he call attention to the nuances of timing and phrasing that helped mobilize support for RU 486. Sakiz followed the old Venetian maxim "The truth but not to everyone." He avoided outright lying and instead maneuvered and dissembled.

The third aspect of balance involves looking beyond the present moment and pursuing balance, not just for the present, but over time. Because the future is unpredictable, a balanced plan of action must be robust across a range of possible scenarios and altered circumstances. Sakiz made only one decision: on introducing RU 486 in France. Decisions about China, the United States, and the rest of Europe were postponed. And the decision on France was only a "temporary suspension." In short, Sakiz made just one move on a very complicated chessboard and waited to see how others would react and what would happen next.

Finally, Sakiz was modest about his and Roussel-Uclaf's roles in the extremely complex decision process for RU 486. He did not try to make final, binding, ethically sound decisions for the many stakeholders—countries, government agencies, medical groups, women's organizations, and churches—that would be affected by the drug. Indeed, he didn't even try to make the entire decision himself. By voting for a temporary suspension, Sakiz simply put the issue in play. Then he worked as a shrewd activist, one among many, and let his country's political authorities make the final decision. This was not only tactically shrewd, it was also morally sound. Final decisions on a product like RU 486—with its extraordinary ethical, political, social, and medical implications—did not belong solely in the hands of a single, relatively small, for-profit organization.

VIRTUE AND *VIRTU*

What do we get by juxtaposing Machiavelli's views on success and *virtu* with Aristotle's views on balance and virtue? At first glance, we have responsible, practical-minded advice for managers facing difficult problems. Aristotle seems to offer a way of domesticating Machiavelli's menacing view of the ethics of public life. The practice of *virtu* is just fine, it seems, so long as it remains within the boundaries of virtue.

But this is far too neat. It ignores Machiavelli's challenge to conventional morality and defines away a central concern of this book: right-versus-right situations. At times, a person in a position of responsibility must do one right thing and leave another undone.

At other times, a person must do something wrong, such as engaging in deception, in order to meet an important ethical obligation. Success and *virtu* sometimes demand what virtue discourages. This is why the veteran leader in *Dirty Hands* asked, "Do you think you can govern innocently?"

In fact, the problem runs even deeper. Virtue and *virtu* are not simply alternative toolkits that managers can take off the shelf and use depending on the circumstances. Aristotle and Machiavelli would agree that they should be, and typically are, character traits, not tactics. A young person—Steve Lewis, for example—chooses a profession. To succeed, as we have seen, he must concentrate his energies, hone particular skills, intensify specific elements of his personality, and think about people and situations in certain ways. Gaining power and responsibility in an organization requires a sustained effort. Leading, changing, and defending an organization demand and instill particular ways of seeing the world and shaping it. A profession becomes a way of life. It demands certain virtues, risks certain vices, and shapes people in particular ways.

Sakiz's career definitely suggests this conclusion. Did he plan each of the steps described in this chapter? Did he dispassionately calculate the odds of each scenario? Was he the grand, far-sighted puppeteer for whom everyone else danced? Of course not. According to press accounts, Sakiz struggled with the decisions, and the anxiety he felt apparently brimmed over at his press conferences. But his life seems to have prepared him to operate instinctively and shrewdly, to muddle and maneuver roughly forward, in exceedingly complex circumstances. Born of Armenian parents in Turkey, Sakiz immigrated to France, where he trained as a scientist and doctor, and then managed a complex company, owned partly by the French government and a huge German conglomerate and linked through strategic alliance to several other large organizations. In all likelihood, this background prepared him to guide his company responsibly and pragmatically through the vortex of the abortion debate. For well or ill, the RU 486 episode revealed and tested the person Sakiz had become through the career he had chosen and the life he had lived.

There is no final reconciliation of virtue and *virtu*. They remain in permanent tension. Managers live and work in two worlds simultaneously. One is a web of responsibilities, commitments, and ethical aspirations. The best guides to this world are the search for balance and the practice of virtue. The other world is an arena of intense, sometimes brutal competition. Here success demands *virtu*.

Often the tensions between these worlds lie dormant. Then managers can simply go about their business. When the tensions erupt, however, in the form of acute conflicts and painful choices, they can exact an awful toll. This is why Abraham Lincoln aged so dramatically during the Civil War years. It is why Chester Barnard used the phrase "moral destruction" to describe how moral conflicts affect executives.

These crucial choices, however painful, do have another side. They are defining moments, in which organizations and their leaders reveal their abiding commitments, test the strength of their ideals, and shape their character. These moments demand creativity, persistence, courage, restraint, shrewdness, and fairness. They demand the capacity to work and live with the inescapable tension between virtue and *virtu*.

As such, these situations are moments of potential greatness. At least this was the conviction of the ethical realist who has remained silent throughout this chapter. Friedrich Nietzsche wrote that "the greatest perhaps also possess great virtues, but in that case also their opposites. I believe that it is precisely through the presence of opposites and the feelings they occasion that the great man, *the bow with great tension*, develops."[13]

9

↔

A Space of Quiet

THE MODERN WORLD SEEMS AT ODDS with much of the guidance offered in this book. Daily life, many people feel, is accelerated and fragmented. Managers everywhere are under pressure to provide action and answers *now*. As a result, when they must choose between right and right, managers often have little opportunity to step back and reflect on the complex issues, personal and professional, that they must somehow resolve.

This is a hazardous situation. Right-versus-right decisions are challenging enough, even when managers have the luxury of thinking them through. The stakes are high: right-versus-right choices are defining moments in which managers reveal, test, and shape— sometimes irrevocably—their values and those of their organizations. These decisions involve difficult conflicts among managers' responsibilities to themselves, to other people in their organizations, and to other groups in society.

Fortunately, responsible managers are unlikely to ignore defining moments entirely, even if their lives are hectic. Right-versus-right decisions call attention to themselves because they pull managers in several different directions simultaneously. Managers know something is amiss; they feel torn. The disquieting question Do you think you can govern innocently? looms in the background.

But what then? If life is a merry-go-round, whirling faster and faster as the carnival music blares, where is the time and space for personal reflection? How do questions like This is my way, where is yours? get the care and consideration they deserve? How can one pursue the "simplicity on the other side of complexity" when complexities lie everywhere? And are there ways to avoid the serious tactical errors, like those that nearly cost Peter Adario his job and his self-esteem, or the deep, permanent regrets, like those the butler Stevens contemplated as his career neared its end? The challenge, in short, is to find ways to keep the immediately important from overwhelming the fundamentally important.

MARCUS AURELIUS

One way to do this is through the advice and example of a man who addressed this challenge head on, in both his writings and his life: This is Marcus Aurelius, the Roman emperor and philosopher—and a distant forebear of *both* the managers and the philosophers we have examined.

Marcus knew full well the cares and responsibilities of practical life because he spent much of his adulthood grappling with almost-overwhelming administrative responsibilities. Between A.D. 161 and 180, he ruled a vast, diverse, unruly empire that spanned much of Europe, North Africa, and the Middle East. Marcus was also Pontifex Maximus, the chief priest of the Roman religion, and the highest judge in the Roman courts. Near the end of his life, when his health was failing, he spent years far from Rome, leading its armies in long campaigns against invading tribes.

Remarkably, this busy, burdened, practical man was also a philosopher. Marcus cared about the ethics of daily life and practical wisdom, not grand theory or systematic knowledge. One commentator describes him this way: "Marcus was a Roman, not greatly drawn to discursive thought, but fascinated by the problems of action, of dealing with people, of adjustment to work, of maintaining serenity in a whirl of exacting business."[1]

For guidance in life, Marcus turned to Stoicism. This school of philosophy, which had originated in Greece four centuries before he lived, was actually more of a religion than a systematic theory, for its principal aim was to provide meaning and direction for everyday life. Stoics sought comfort in divine providence, prized virtue and reason, sought liberation from passions, and tried not to concern themselves with matters they could not control.

How did Marcus Aurelius combine the life of action with the spirit of reflection? How did he take the long view of the urgent tasks of the present moment? The answers lie in his personal journal. During the last years of his life, Marcus kept an informal record of his reflections, observations, and self-criticisms. He wrote for himself, not for the eyes of others. He wanted to understand who he was and how he should work and live. Marcus called the journal *To Himself*, and only centuries later did it come to be called *Meditations*.

Here is a description of Marcus, seated in a large tent, writing by candlelight during a military campaign:

> *When the camp had gone to sleep, the emperor, who was late to bed and early to rise, sat at his table and took stock, not of battles, sieges, and fortunes, of which there is little mention, but of himself, his state of mind, his lapses from justice or from speaking the truth or from command of his temper. He used these night hours to conjure up the ideals he had set before himself as a man and as a ruler of men, to see them more clearly, to consider what they demanded of him, to consider what he was in the light of what he might have been and in reason ought to be.*[2]

The life and thoughts of Marcus Aurelius suggest three lessons for escaping the tyranny of the here-and-now and making the guidance in this book as concrete and useful as possible.

MOMENTS OF SERENITY

The first lesson Marcus Aurelius might suggest for managers has nothing to do with work. In fact, its focus is on *not* working. Marcus's advice would be to work hard to create moments of serenity. Again and again, throughout *Meditations*, Marcus reminds himself to slow down and step back, to withdraw and reflect. He writes, "Are you distracted by outward cares? Then allow yourself a space of quiet, wherein you can add to your knowledge of the Good and learn to curb your restlessness."[3] He tells himself "Nowhere can a man find a quieter or more untroubled retreat than in his own soul."[4] And, again, "Avail yourself often, then, of this retirement, and so continually renew yourself."[5]

This talk of retirement and retreat may sound otherworldly and monkish. It may suggest someone without the stomach for the hard work of trying to make a practical difference in the world. But there is no indication that Marcus ever shirked the duties and cares of his position. He ruled until his death—and may actually have hastened it—because he refused, to the very end, to lay down any of the duties and burdens of his office.

Marcus believed that serenity could protect him from the hazard of overimmersion, of losing himself and his bearings in the unending stream of life's tasks. Serenity was also his antidote for the incessant clamor, unending petitions, and elaborate intrigues of court life. Marcus sought not to hide from life, but to renew himself to live it better—to understand his responsibilities and prepare to meet them, psychologically, emotionally, and spiritually.

Were Marcus Aurelius alive today, he might well ask managers whether they have, somewhere in their lives, a counterpart to his tent, with its candle and plain table. He would be inquiring (discreetly and quietly—for he was, by all accounts, a gentle soul) not about a physical location, but about a mental retreat where they could reflect and renew themselves. Marcus might well be astonished and concerned at how infrequently the men and women who shoulder so many of the world's responsibilities remove themselves from other people, agendas, deadlines, telephones, and computers and simply sit for a while and examine themselves, their lives, their thoughts and feelings.

Here, for example, are the recollections of a widely respected executive, shortly after his retirement as chairman of a very successful Fortune 500 firm:

I dropped out for two months last year. I went to Colorado and took off my watch; I just dropped off. I was astonished at how much stress I'd been living under for the last 35 years. The stress just peeled off and peeled off and peeled off and the adrenaline drained out of me. . . . I've got to learn to live at a much lower adrenaline level and be happy with myself. I've got to learn not to be totally addicted to a schedule of rapid interaction with others, to be addicted to how others see me, something which, unfortunately, is extremely important in terms of running a business.[6]

Marcus would urge the men and women who recognize themselves in this passage to find or make some time that is genuinely their own, time when they are not serving as nodes in a network of tasks and relationships. His concern would be that busy managers find ways to create "a space of quiet" in their lives.

THE SEARCH FOR LIVED TRUTHS

Marcus's second lesson is implicit in scores of entries in *Meditations*. He believed that moments of serenity and reflection should be used, in part, as preparation for the tasks of everyday life and work, and for the occasional, often crucial challenges we have called "defining moments." Marcus filled his journal with reminders, warnings, exhortations, and suggestions. They reveal a mind preoccupied with the question of how to live, think, work, lead, and act. Even when Marcus reflects, as he often does, on the nature of the universe, the fate of humankind, or his own mortality, he usually draws lessons for his life in the here-and-now.

How did Marcus use his periods of reflection to prepare himself to meet his responsibilities? Perhaps the most valuable part of the answer lies—albeit in disguise—in the first chapter of *Meditations*. Here Marcus expresses gratitude, one by one, to more than a dozen people, each of whom influenced his life. He begins with his grandfather, thanking him for his example of "courtesy and serenity." Near the end of the chapter, just before he concludes by thanking the gods, Marcus takes two pages to describe all that he learned from his father.

This chapter can easily be overlooked. It appears, at first, to be simply a catalogue of dutiful acknowledgments. But there is much more to it. The chapter is an example of a powerful and practical way of taking the guidance offered in this book—or, for that matter, any guidance on how to live—and making it one's own. To prepare for the challenges of the day, both great and small, Marcus worked hard to learn all he could from the lives and experiences of people he knew well.

What Marcus searched for, his first chapter suggests, were lived truths, ethical standards validated in everyday life, and virtues forged in life's crucibles. Marcus relies heavily on phrases like "he showed me" and "he was living proof" and "through him I came to see" when he describes how he learned from others. He examined how people actually lived and acted, not what they said in their speeches, credos, or statements of moral principle. This search for lived truths is the basis for Marcus Aurelius's second lesson. He would advise managers to work very hard to become astute, probing, insightful observers of the lives, efforts, and experiences of the people around them—particularly managers who have faced defining moments and resolved them well.

Experience places flesh-and-blood case studies before almost every manager. These are valuable opportunities for learning how other managers—in one's own industry, in jobs that one may some-day hold—have found ways to resolve some of the moral dilemmas of management. In fact, all of the questions presented in this book can be rephrased just slightly and used as guides for reflecting on the real-life case studies that almost every organization offers to people who look for them. For example, each of the personal questions raised by decisions like Steve Lewis's can serve as a lens for carefully examining the issues of moral identity that other managers have had to resolve. Used in this way, the questions take the following form: How do managers I know seem to be answering Nietzsche's injunction to "Become who you are"? What values have the deepest roots in their lives? How did their feelings and intuitions define their right-versus-right conflict? How did they gain and use the power they had?

The Steve Lewis case provides a glimpse of this approach to the personal elements of defining moments. Before making his decision about the St. Louis trip, he thought about the example his parents had set, particularly when the restaurant refused to seat them. He also tried to look at his decision through the eyes of Andy, his mentor. If Lewis had more time, he could have asked other African-American analysts how they had handled similar situations. Better still, he would have discussed their experiences with them and with Andy *before* he was asked about St. Louis, and he would have thought seriously about how he might respond to situations like theirs. The minicase studies of the other analysts could have provided him with questions, lessons, and warnings. Each was a chance to learn from the experiences of people who had embarked on the same professional path he had chosen.

The questions about defining moments for organizations—the issues with which Peter Adario struggled—can also be used as lenses for learning. Used this way, the questions become: What ethical values have the managers whom I know and admire chosen as guides for their organizations? What were the competing interpretations that had to be overcome? How did they translate these into "cash value" for the people whose support they needed? How did they orchestrate a process that made particular values become the truth for their organization? When and how did they play to win? How did they divert or block their adversaries?

Unfortunately, when Peter Adario prepared to resolve the dilemma he faced, he relied on a single case, his idealized recollection of the Tylenol story. He did not draw on events and decisions of his own life or that he knew from close observation. Nor did he draw on his wife's experience, even though she had left two jobs because her employers had failed to address work-family issues.

Finally, there are the questions that ask managers to look beyond the boundaries of their organizations, such as the questions Edouard Sakiz had to resolve in the case of RU 486. These, too, can be recast as devices for reflection and learning. Used this way, the questions become: What managers, in my experience, have thought creatively and imaginatively about their organization's role in society and its responsibilities to stakeholders? How did they secure their positions and the strength and stability of their organizations? When and how did they play the lion? When and how did they play the fox? How did they strike balances, morally and practically, as they moved toward their objectives?

Marcus's second lesson thus encourages managers to look beyond questions—Aristotle's, Machiavelli's, Nietzsche's, James's, or anyone else's—and search for answers, in the form of rich, detailed stories of actual managers, their dilemmas and choices, and the consequences of their actions. This is a way of understanding the power of these questions and preparing, as best one can, to answer them well when a right-versus-right conflict arises.

THE IMAGINED BEST LIFE

Part of the enduring beauty of *Meditations* is its sense of the eternal. This is why, for centuries, this slender volume has appealed to men and women with widely differing religious and philosophical backgrounds. Although Marcus Aurelius cared deeply about preparing to live well, during the next day or even the next hour, he also managed to place his day-to-day concerns in the context of his whole life, and his whole life in the context of eternity.

For example, some of the passages in *Meditations* suggest that Marcus was tempted, at least by his own standards, to dwell on his reputation and role in history. Here is what he tells himself, to discourage this tendency:

> *Does some bubble of fame torment you? Then fix your gaze on swift oblivion, on the gulf of infinity this way and that, on the empty rattle of plaudits and the undiscriminating fickleness of professed applause and the narrow range within which you are circumscribed. The whole earth is but a point, your habitation but a tiny nook thereon.*[7]

Reflecting on the meaning of particular decisions for their lives is especially important for managers facing defining moments. Faced with an urgent, practical problem, there is a serious risk that the tactical, pragmatic, action-oriented, politically astute questions suggested by Machiavelli and James will overmaster the more personal, longer-term, and intangible questions suggested by Aristotle and

Nietzsche. For Aristotle, the basic question about ethics was What is a good life? It is easy to lose sight of this vital perspective on an important choice when the pressures and complexities of the moment fill up the entire horizon.

It is true that the present is our only opportunity to think, feel, choose, and act. A practical man, Marcus knew this well. "Were you to live three thousand years," he writes, "or even thirty thousand, remember that the sole life which a man can lose is that which he is living at the moment."[8] Later, he tells himself "that man lives only in the present, in this fleeting instant: all the rest of his life is either past and gone, or not yet revealed."[9]

But Marcus, like Aristotle, also understood the value of looking up from the urgent tasks of the moment and placing them in the larger context of the life he wanted to live. The first chapter of *Meditations* does this in a distinctive way. Marcus does not simply describe people he admired and vow to live his life as they did. Instead, he praises each of them for particular aspects of their lives and personalities. He picks and chooses, admiring particular people for particular virtues, skills, and traits.

One reason for his selective approach may have been that Marcus was thinking about people he knew well. He had been their student or son or brother or friend, so he knew their failings, imperfections, and vices. This is probably one reason why he sought to emulate only certain facets of their lives. Another reason is that Marcus understood the unpredictability of life and the strong likelihood that he would face decisions and situations that his parents, grandparents, and teachers had not encountered. He was a different person, ruling in a new and troubled era, embarking on a different voyage. Hence, he focused on the navigation devices—the traits that guided these individuals through the challenges of life and work—rather than on the maps that his guiding figures had followed.

There is also a third reason—perhaps the most important—why Marcus did not simply pick one hero or exemplar and then vow to live as this role model had. The reason is that Marcus wanted to live his own life and not replicate someone else's. By picking out certain facets of others' characters, he was creating, actively, consciously, and in vivid detail, his own image of a good person and a good life.

As a faithful Stoic, Marcus believed that people should live "according to nature." But nature, in his mind, was not a cookie cutter that stamped out a single model of a good person or a good life. Rather, as one authority on Marcus Aurelius puts it:

> *Marcus would have had some sympathy with a movement of recent days that is sometimes an excuse for self-absorption, but at its best is the main business of life, the search for one's own identity. That identity may not be easy to discover. Every man, according to Marcus, is a little eruption of Deity, "a bright shoot of everlastingness," so that his duty in a deep sense lies in becoming himself.* [10]

Marcus created a mental sketch or collage of the virtues, skills, activities, commitments, habits, and values that he prized and wanted to make his own. The composite picture Marcus created for himself includes ways of being a friend, showing affection to children, dealing with flatterers, showing courtesy, practicing self-control, worshiping the gods, and serving the community. The examples belong to others, but the combination is Marcus's own. Thus he begins *Meditations* with the picture of an "imagined best life"—an image of the life he wanted to live. [11] Then, in the rest of his journal, Marcus reflects on how well he is living this life.

Marcus would likely ask managers today if they have reflected carefully and creatively on their personal versions of the imagined best life. He would advise them to select, drawing on their experience of life, the combination of character traits that forms their image of a responsible, satisfying life as a person and as a manager. This image or ideal, he would tell them, can help them get their bearings, stay their course, and bind their daily work to larger ends and purposes.

THE ART OF REFLECTION

Marcus Aurelius evolved his own way of melding work, life, and reflection. His particular approach—the journal, the late-night solitude—fit his life and personality. But his approach is not for everyone. The ends Marcus pursued are far more important than the means he adopted. What he sought, above all, were retreat and renewal, lived truths, and the image of the life he wanted to live.

Others who would follow his example need to seek their own approach to the art of reflection. In doing so, they will be embarking on a path that men and women have been following for millennia— for, in fundamental ways, Marcus's *Meditations* are the ancient counterpart to Nietzsche's contemporary plea "Become who you are."

Consider the following passage, in which Nietzsche describes his "myth of eternal recurrence." It is his advice for reflecting on the imagined best life. His poetic passage is worth reading aloud and slowly:

> *What if a demon crept after you one day or night in your loneliest solitude and said to you, "This life, as you live it now and have lived it, you will have to live again and again, times without number; and there will be nothing new in it, but every pain and every joy and every thought and sigh and all the unspeakably small and great in your life must return to you, and everything in the same series and sequences—and in the same way this spider and this moonlight among the trees, and in the same way this moment and I myself."*[12]

Nietzsche evokes a late-night moment of utter stillness, perhaps like the moments in which Marcus Aurelius, working by candlelight, composed *Meditations*. Work has ended, and the buzzing of daily life has ceased. It is then, Nietzsche suggests, that a person should contemplate the prospect of making a particular decision or living a certain kind of life, again and again, forever. Like Marcus Aurelius, Nietzsche is suggesting a way to take a moment, a choice, a commitment and place it in the context of a person's whole life.

In this way, Nietzsche is pursuing the same goal as Marcus Aurelius and the other philosophers to whom we have turned. All sought to help thoughtful people make difficult choices—in ways that stand the test of time and express standards and values, rooted in the experience and wisdom of others, that they have made their own.

Notes

Chapter 1

1. Jean Paul Sartre, *Dirty Hands*, in *No Exit and Three Other Plays* (New York: Vintage International, 1989), 218.
2. Chester A. Barnard, *The Functions of the Executive* (Cambridge, MA: Harvard University Press, 1982), 278.
3. A thoughtful overview and analysis of the dirty hands problem, as well as its intellectual history, is Kenneth I. Winston, "Necessity and Choice in Political Ethics: Varieties of Dirty Hands," in Daniel E. Wueste, ed., *Professional Ethics and Social Responsibility* (London: Rowman and Littlefield Publishers, 1994), 37–66.

Chapter 2

1. This phrase is from a classic article on middle managers: Hugo E. R. Uyterhoeven, "General Managers in the Middle," *Harvard Business Review*, March–April 1972, 84.
2. This phrase appears in G. B. Richardson, "The Organization of Industry," *Economic Journal* 82 (1972): 883.

Chapter 3

1. The most recent comprehensive study of company ethics programs is Rebecca Goodell, *Ethics in American Business: Policies, Programs and*

Perceptions (Washington, DC: Ethics Resources Center, 1994). A thoughtful review of studies of similar programs appears in Donald L. McCabe, Linda Klebe Trevino, and Kenneth D. Butterfield, "The Influence of Collegiate and Corporate Codes of Conduct on Ethics-Related Behavior in the Workplace," *Business Ethics Quarterly*, October 1996, 461–476.

2. Steven Kerr, "Risky Business: The New Pay Game," *Fortune*, 22 July 1996, 94.
3. Scholars have confirmed what these managers learned from experience. The *Financial Analysts Journal* recently examined the fairness of rules against insider trading. The authors found it necessary to use seven different definitions of "financial market fairness" to justify these rules. Moreover, they found that specialists in finance disagreed about the weights that should be assigned to each of these different versions of fairness. See Hersh Shefrin and Meir Statman, "Ethics, Fairness and Efficiency in Financial Markets," *Financial Analysts Journal* (November–December 1993): 22.
4. Goodell, 1–5.
5. William James, *Pragmatism* (Buffalo, NY: Prometheus Books, 1991), 13.
6. Milton Friedman, "The Social Responsibility of Business Is to Increase Its Profits," *New York Times Magazine*, 13 September 1970, 33.
7. E. Merrick Dodd, Jr., "For Whom Are Corporate Managers Trustees?" *Harvard Law Review*, 8 May 1932, 1145–1163.
8. American Law Institute, *Principles of Corporate Governance: Analysis and Recommendation*, vol. 1 (St. Paul, MN: American Law Institute Publishers, 1994), 438–440.
9. Jay Lorsch, *Pawns or Potentates* (Boston: Harvard Business School Press, 1989).
10. For a historical and analytical overview of these issues, see Eric W. Orts, "Beyond Shareholders: Interpreting Corporate Constituency Statutes," *George Washington Law Review*, November 1992, 6–132.
11. See Alasdair MacIntyre, *After Virtue* (Notre Dame, IN: University of Notre Dame Press, 1984), 51–78.
12. The political philosopher Michael Walzer has observed that "the first impulse of the philosopher is to resist the displays of history, the world of appearances, and a search for some underlying unity: a short list of basic goods, quickly abstracted to a single good; and the philosopher himself standing, symbolically at least, at a single decision point." See Michael Walzer, *Spheres of Justice* (New York: Basic Books,

1983), 4. This approach is a standard way of teaching professional ethics. A typical textbook in the field begins with summaries of the moral philosophy of John Stuart Mill, Immanuel Kant, and others. Then the rest of the book provides case studies to which students apply these theories.

13. MacIntyre, *After Virtue*, 6.

14. In recent years, hospitals have begun relying on ethicists, typically with training in moral philosophy, as consultants on difficult issues. Anecdotal evidence suggests that they make valued contributions, but studies raise doubts. One study asked medical ethics consultants how they would handle several situations involving life-prolonging treatment for patients in persistent vegetative states. The authors found a general agreement among the consultants for only one of seven vignettes. This was a case of a patient whose personal directive and whose family had agreed that life-prolonging treatment should be stopped if the person fell into a persistent vegetative state. In the words of the study's authors, the "responses to the other vignettes varied considerably." See Ellen Fox and Carol Stocking, "Ethics Consultants' Recommendation for Life-Prolonging Treatment of Patients in a Persistent Vegetative State," *Journal of the American Medical Association* (1 December 1993): 2578.

15. Among British and American philosophers, the most influential versions of this criticism of utilitarianism and Kantianism are Bernard William's essays "Moral Luck" and "Persons, Character, and Morality" in Bernard Williams, *Moral Luck: Philosophical Papers, 1973–1980* (Cambridge, UK: Cambridge University Press, 1981).

16. David Hume is quoted in Kenneth Boulding, "The Economics of Knowledge and the Knowledge of Economics," *American Economic Review*, May 1966, 1.

Chapter 4

1. William H. Gilman, ed., *Selected Writings of Ralph Waldo Emerson* (New York: Penguin Books, 1983), 264.

2. See, for example, Will Durant, *The Story of Philosophy* (New York: Simon & Schuster, 1961), 41.

3. These quotations were taken from lengthy interviews conducted in 1992 with 35 MBA candidates. The aim of the research was to determine what men and women in the early years of their careers think about ethical issues. The sleep test appeared frequently in their

explanations of how they had resolved ethical dilemmas at work. See Joseph L. Badaracco, Jr., and Allen P. Webb, "Business Ethics: A View from the Trenches," *California Management Review* (Winter 1995): 8–28.

4. Douglas Coupland, *Generation X* (New York: St. Martin's Press, 1991), 186.

5. Kenichi Ohmai, "Letter from Japan," *Harvard Business Review*, May–June 1995, 161.

6. The omissions seem to be no accident. Large-scale studies indicate the same pattern. For example, a 1992 Gallup survey of more than 1,000 teenagers and young adults indicated that nearly all young people believe in a God of at least some universal spirit. But the young people were basically "turned off" by established churches; only 1 teenager in 4 expressed a high degree of confidence in organized religion. The survey noted "a glaring lack of knowledge of the Ten Commandments" and basic religious tenets. George H. Gallup International Institute, *The Religious Life of Young Americans* (Princeton, NJ: George H. Gallup International Institute, 1992), 4–12.

7. These statistics appear in Coupland, *Generation X*, 186–187.

8. Hemingway makes this statement at the beginning of his long treatise on bullfighting. On this basis, he concludes that bullfighting is moral. He writes that he feels "very fine" while he watches bullfights and "very fine" afterward, and this seems to settle the issue in his mind. See Ernest Hemingway, *Death in the Afternoon* (New York: Simon & Schuster, 1996), 4.

9. Thomas Keneally, *Schindler's List* (New York: Simon & Schuster, 1982).

10. Friedrich Nietzsche, *Thus Spake Zarathustra* (London: G. Allen & Unwin, 1967), 149.

11. In this vein, James Q. Wilson's recent book *The Moral Sense* compiles evidence from nearly every academic field to support his conclusion that human beings have a "persistent but fragile disposition" to think in moral terms. See James Q. Wilson, *The Moral Sense* (New York: The Free Press, 1993), xv, 225–251. Among popular accounts of evolutionary theory, Wilson's is fairly optimistic. A less-sanguine view is articulated in Robert Wright's highly regarded book *The Moral Animal*, which is a study of the social implications of evolutionary biology. Wright concludes, "Chronically subjecting ourselves to a true and bracing moral scrutiny, and adjusting our behavior accordingly, is not something we are designed for. We are potentially

moral animals—which is more than any other animal can say—but we aren't naturally moral animals. To be moral animals, we must realize how thoroughly we aren't."

12. A full account of Gage's accident and an analysis from the perspective of modern neuroscience can be found in Antonio R. Damasio, *Descartes' Error* (New York: G. P. Putnam's Sons, 1994).

13. Robert N. Bellah, *Habits of the Heart* (New York: Harper & Row, 1985), 3–84, 333–334.

14. Another way of describing this realistic approach is called PMPR, the principle of minimal psychological realism. Behind the nomenclature is an eminently sound suggestion: "Make sure when constructing a moral theory or projecting a moral ideal that the character, decision process, and behavior prescribed are possible . . . for creatures like us." See Owen Flanagan, *Varieties of Moral Personality: Ethics and Psychological Realism* (Cambridge, MA: Harvard University Press, 1991), 32.

15. Martha C. Nussbaum, *Love's Knowledge: Essays on Philosophy and Literature* (New York: Oxford University Press, 1990), 42.

16. See Stuart Hampshire, *Morality and Conflict* (Cambridge, MA: Harvard University Press, 1983), 103.

17. Those in search of precise criteria will find even stronger grounds for frustration, because it isn't difficult to think of additional criteria for a sound moral decision. For example, in his book *A Theory of Justice*, the eminent contemporary philosopher John Rawls discusses "considered judgments" about moral issues and writes that they can be taken into account in circumstances in which "the more common excuses and explanations for making a mistake do not obtain." These include self-interest in the outcome, strong hesitation about a judgment, a feeling of fear or upset. See John Rawls, *A Theory of Justice* (Cambridge, MA: Harvard University Press, 1971), 46–48. No doubt there are still other criteria. There may well be no final complete list of criteria, nor criteria for determining which criteria apply in a particular case.

18. Two outstanding works on the relationships between literature and ethics are Wayne C. Booth, *The Company We Keep: An Ethics of Fiction* (Berkeley: University of California Press, 1988), especially 49–81 and 265–293, and Nussbaum, *Love's Knowledge*, especially 3–53 and 261–269.

19. William James, *Pragmatism* (Buffalo, NY: Prometheus Books, 1991), 9–10.

Chapter 5

1. Kazuo Ishiguro, *The Remains of the Day* (New York: Alfred Knopf, 1989). The passages in this chapter are taken from this edition of the book.
2. See Paul Binding, "Passing the Butler," *The Listener*, 25 May 1989, 25.
3. John Dewey, *Ethics* (New York: Henry Holt and Company, 1932), 316.
4. Chester Barnard, *The Functions of the Executive* (Cambridge, MA: Harvard University Press, 1982), 267.
5. Michael J. Sandel, "The Procedural Republic and the Unencumbered Self," *Political Theory* (February 1984): 86–87.
6. Aristotle, *The Basic Works of Aristotle*, ed. Richard McKeon (New York: Random House, 1941), 1130.
7. Aristotle, *Nichomachean Ethics*, trans. Terence Irwin (Indianapolis: Hackett Publishing Company, 1985), 35.
8. John Dewey, *Ethics*, 317.
9. Ishiguro, *The Remains of the Day*, 179.

Chapter 6

1. Alasdair MacIntyre, *After Virtue* (Notre Dame, IN: University of Notre Dame Press, 1984), 114.
2. Walter Kaufmann, *Nietzsche: Philosopher, Psychologist, and Antichrist* (Princeton, NJ: Princeton University Press, 1974), 45.
3. For a thorough debunking of the image of Nietzsche as a proto-Nazi, see Kaufmann, *Nietzsche*, 42–46, 284–306.
4. It is nearly impossible to characterize the vast literature on Nietzsche, which numbers hundreds of books currently in print and thousands of articles, nor the range of scholarly and popular writing his ideas have influenced. Part of the problem is that there have been too many "Nietzsches." A brief and highly oversimplified overview of them might begin with the evil Nietzsche created by his sister, his brother-in-law, and the Nazis; then move to the Nietzsche rehabilitated by Kaufmann and other scholars as a fertile source of insight for philosophers, psychologists, and literary critics; then yet another evil Nietzsche—the destroyer of all objective values portrayed in a *Time* magazine cover story three decades ago and more recently in *The Closing of the American Mind*, the best-selling critique of American higher education (see Allan Bloom, *The Closing of the American Mind* [New York: Touchstone Books, 1988]); to yet another

Nietzsche, defanged and domesticated, who emerges in Peter Berkowitz, *Nietzsche: The Ethics of an Immoralist* (Cambridge, MA: Harvard University Press, 1995).

5. Friedrich Nietzsche, *Thus Spake Zarathustra* (London: G. Allen & Unwin, 1967), 281.

6. Friedrich Nietzsche, *The Gay Science* (New York: Random House, 1974), 232.

7. This passage and the other below are from Sophocles, *Antigone*, trans. E. F. Watling (London: Penguin Books, 1974), 126–162.

8. William James, *Pragmatism* (Buffalo, NY: Prometheus Books, 1991), 126.

9. MacIntyre, *After Virtue*, 220. Stuart Hampshire makes a similar point, writing, " 'This is how I feel and this is how I have always felt: to change now would be to repudiate my past, and I find nothing unjust or harmful in the practice.' These are justifications in a moral context, all of which appeal to the agent's sense of his own identity and character as a person and of his history, which partly determines his sense of identity." See Stuart Hampshire, *Morality and Conflict* (Cambridge, MA: Harvard University Press, 1983), 8. Michael Sandel, in a similar vein, describes what he calls "constitutive commitments," which define a person so completely that turning away from them would call into question the person that one was. See Michael J. Sandel, "The Procedural Republic and the Unencumbered Self," *Political Theory* (February 1984): 86.

10. Calvin Trillin, *Remembering Denny* (New York: Warner Books, 1993), 25.

11. Nietzsche, *Thus Spake Zarathustra*, 241.

12. Friedrich Nietzsche, *Beyond Good and Evil* (New York: Vintage Press, 1966), 44.

Chapter 7

1. See Gerald E. Myers, *Williams James* (New Haven, CT: Yale University Press, 1986), 20.

2. Ibid., 31.

3. Ibid. Nietzsche held a similar view. In *The Will to Power*, he wrote "Against positivism, which halts at phenomena—'There are only facts'—I would say: 'No, facts is precisely what there are not, only interpretations.' " See Friedrich Nietzsche, *The Will to Power* (New York: Vintage, 1968), 267.

4. William James, *Pragmatism* (Buffalo, NY: Prometheus Books, 1991), 107.
5. Morton Mintz, "Drug Fiends: Even Inside Johnson & Johnson, Public Safety Can Take a Back Seat to Profits," *Washington Monthly*, December 1991, 20.
6. Kevin Kelly and Joseph Weber, "When a Rival's Trade Secrets Cross Your Desk," *Business Week*, 20 May 1991, 48.
7. William M. Carley, "Court Papers Detail Ortho's Retin-A Deception," *Wall Street Journal*, 1 March 1995, B1.
8. James, *Pragmatism*, 88, 36.
9. Ibid., 20.
10. Ibid., 89.
11. Friedrich Nietzsche, *The Will to Power* (New York: Vintage Press, 1968), 418.
12. Richard S. Tedlow, *James Burke: A Career in American Business* (Boston: Harvard Business School, 1990), videocassette 9-890-513.
13. Niccolo Machiavelli, *The Prince*, book 25.
14. Nietzsche, *The Will to Power*, 188.
15. Ibid.
16. The phrase "midlife reconsideration" is used by W. Jackson Bate to summarize a central theme in his biography of Samuel Johnson. See W. Jackson Bate, *Samuel Johnson* (New York: Harcourt Brace Jovanovich, 1977), especially 229–367.

Chapter 8

1. Steven Greenhouse, "Maker Says Pressure Could Revive Abortion Pill," *New York Times*, 28 October 1988, A9.
2. Ibid.
3. Ibid.
4. Isaiah Berlin, "The Originality of Machiavelli," in Henry Hardy, ed., *Against the Current* (New York: The Viking Press, 1980), 39.
5. Ibid., 66.
6. Ibid., 59.
7. J. H. Plumb, *The Italian Renaissance* (New York: American Heritage, 1961), 18.
8. Niccolo Machiavelli, *The Prince*, 142.
9. Ibid.
10. Ibid., 144.
11. Aristotle, *Ethics* (London: Penguin Books, 1976), 94.

12. Stuart Hampshire, *Morality and Conflict* (Cambridge, MA: Harvard University Press, 1983) 38.

13. Friedrich Nietzsche, *The Will to Power* (New York: Vintage, 1968), 507.

Chapter 9

1. Brand Blanshard, *Four Reasonable Men* (Middletown, CT: Wesleyan University Press, 1984), 41.

2. Ibid., 4.

3. Marcus Aurelius, *Meditations* (London: Penguin Books, 1964), 47.

4. Ibid., 63.

5. Ibid.

6. Bhavin Shah, "The Life and Times of Tom Urban," *Under Cover* (Fall 1996): 26.

7. Blanshard, *Four Reasonable Men*, 44.

8. Marcus Aurelius, *Meditations* (London: Penguin Books, 1964), 49.

9. Ibid., 69.

10. Blanshard, *Four Reasonable Men*, 24.

11. The phrase "imagined best life" is Stuart Hampshire's, which he uses to explain his conception of Aristotle's ethics. See Stuart Hampshire, *Morality and Conflict* (Cambridge, MA: Harvard University Press, 1983), 19.

12. Friedrich Nietzsche, *The Gay Science* (New York: Vintage Press, 1974), 341.

Index

About the Author

Joseph L. Badaracco, Jr., is the John Shad Professor of Business Ethics at Harvard Business School. He has taught courses on strategy, general management, business-government relations, and business ethics in the School's MBA and executive programs. Badaracco is a graduate of St. Louis University; Oxford University, where he was a Rhodes scholar; and Harvard Business School, where he earned an MBA and a doctorate.

Badaracco has written two other books on manager's ethical responsibilities: *Leadership and the Quest for Integrity* (with Richard Ellsworth) and *Business Ethics: Roles and Responsibilities*. He is also the author of *Loading the Dice*, a study of business-government relations in five countries, and *The Knowledge Link*, a study of international strategic alliances. These books have been translated into eight languages.